Achieving QTS
Reflective Reader: Primary Science

D0588156

Achieving QTS: Reflective Readers

Reflective Reader: Primary Professional Studies
Sue Kendall-Seatter
ISBN-13: 978 1 84445 033 6 ISBN-10: 1 84445 033 3

Reflective Reader: Secondary Professional Studies
Simon Hoult
ISBN-13: 978 1 84445 034 3 ISBN-10: 1 84445 034 1

Reflective Reader: Primary English
Andrew Lambirth
ISBN-13: 978 1 84445 035 0 ISBN-10: 1 84445 035 X

Reflective Reader: Primary Mathematics
Louise O'Sullivan, Andrew Harris, Margaret Sangster, Jon Wild, Gina Donaldson and Gill Bottle
ISBN-13: 978 1 84445 036 7 ISBN-10: 1 84445 036 8

Reflective Reader: Primary Science
Judith Roden
ISBN-13: 978 1 84445 037 4 ISBN-10: 1 84445 037 6

Reflective Reader: Primary Special Educational Needs
Sue Soan
ISBN-13: 978 1 84445 038 1 ISBN-10: 1 84445 038 4

Achieving QTS

Reflective Reader
Primary Science

Judith Roden

Learning Matters

First published in 2005 by Learning Matters Ltd

British Library Cataloguing in Publication Data
A CIP record for this book is available from the British Library.

ISBN-13: 978 1 84445 037 4
ISBN-10: 1 84445 037 6

Cover design by Topics – The Creative Partnerhsip
Project management by Deer Park Productions
Typeset by PDQ Typesetting Ltd
Printed and bound in Great Britain by Bell & Bain Ltd, Glasgow

Learning Matters Ltd
33 Southernhay East
Exeter EX1 1NX
Tel: 01392 215560
Email: info@learningmatters.co.uk
www.learningmatters.co.uk

Contents

Introduction   1

1 Science and school science   6

2 Science as a creative activity   20

3 The role of practical work   33

4 Scientific enquiry   43

5 Children's ideas   56

6 Grouping children for science   70

7 Formative assessment   84

8 Summative assessment   97

References   117

Index   120

Introduction

The series

The *Reflective Reader* series supports the *Achieving QTS* series by providing relevant and topical theory that underpins the reflective learning and practice of primary and secondary ITT trainees.

Each book includes extracts from classic and current publications and documents. These extracts are supported by analysis, pre- and post-reading activities, links to the QTS Standards, a practical implications section, links to other titles in the *Achieving QTS* series and suggestions for further reading.

Integrating theory and practice, the *Reflective Reader* series is specifically designed to encourage trainees and practising teachers to develop the skill and habit of reflecting on their own practice, engaging with relevant theory and identify opportunities to apply theory to improve their teaching skills.

The process of educating individuals is broader than the specific areas of educational theory, research and practice. All humans are educated, socially, politically and culturally. In all but a few cases humans co-exist with other humans and are educated to do so. The position of an individual in society is determined by the nature and quality of the educational process. As a person grows up, emerging from childhood into adulthood, their social and political status is dependent on the educational process. For every task, from eating and sleeping to reading and writing, whether instinctive or learnt, the knowledge and experience gained through the process of education is critical. Humans are educated, consciously and subconsciously, from birth. Education is concerned with the development of individual autonomy, the understanding of which has been generated by educational, sociological, psychological and philosophical theories.

The position of the teacher in this context is ambivalent. In practice each teacher will have some knowledge of theory but may not have had the opportunity to engage with theories that can inform and improve their practice.

In this series, the emphasis is on theory. The authors guide the student to analyse practice within a theoretical framework provided by a range of texts. Through examining why we do what we do and how we do it the reader will be able to relate theory to practice. The series covers primary and secondary professional issues, subject areas and topics. There are also explicit links to Qualifying to Teach Standards (QTS) that will enable both trainees and teachers to improve and develop their subject knowledge.

Each book provides focused coverage of subjects and topics and each extract is accompanied by support material to help trainees and teachers to engage with the extract, draw out the implications for classroom practice and to develop as a reflective practitioner.

While the series is aimed principally at students, it will also be relevant to practitioners in the classroom and staffroom. Each book includes guidance, advice and examples on:

- the knowledge, understanding, theory and practice needed to achieve QTS status;
- how to relate knowledge, theory and practice to a course of study;
- self reflection and analysis through personal responses and reading alone;
- developing approaches to sharing views with colleagues and fellow students.

Readers will develop their skills in relating theory to practice through:

- preparatory reading;
- analysis;
- personal responses;
- practical implications and activities;
- further reading.

Primary science

You may well already feel at ease teaching science: if so, this book will provide you with much food for thought. On the other hand, you may be one of the many people who have a reluctance to teach science either because of your own experience of science or because of its practical nature. If this is the case, this book should help you to understand teaching science in the primary sector better.

This book will be a reference and reflection resource for you as you train to teach science or develop science in your primary classroom. It is designed to reflect key areas of study and development, and draw out issues derived from the structure of the complementary text *Achieving QTS : Primary Science: Teaching Theory and Practice* (Sharp *et al*, Learning Matters, 2002).

The QTS Standards developed since 2002 emphasise the development of professional values and practice. At the core is your ability to reflect and evaluate your own practice and that of others around you. With science this implies the need to tease out, reflect on, question and interrogate the reasons and motives for the inclusion of particular aspects of practice that otherwise might be taken for granted.

Years of debate among science educators have led to a clear general consensus about what science is and how it should be represented in primary schools. The National Curriculum broadly reflects this view, in that science as a body of knowledge and as a way of working feature highly at Key Stages 1 and 2. However, for a variety of reasons, there is often a mismatch between intended practice and practice in action.

In the busy rush of the primary classroom, it is easy to accept without question aspects of common practice in science teaching. There is a great need for trainees and practising teachers to be aware of the issues in order not only to understand the need for change but also to influence and implement change. This requires you to *reflect in action* and also to *reflect on action*.

This book will help you to:

- engage with the issues at a theoretical level with reference to key texts in primary science;
- explore the teaching of science in the primary stage of education;
- reflect on your own principles and development as a teacher and consider how this impacts on your work in the classroom.

Each chapter is structured around the key reflective prompts **why**, **what** and **how**. Each prompt is linked to a short extract. You will:

- read a short analysis of the extract;
- provide a personal response;
- consider the practical implications

and have links to:

- supporting reading;
- the QTS Standards.

A note on extracts

Where possible, extracts are reproduced in full but of necessity many have had to be cut. References to other sources embedded within the extracts are not included in this book. Please refer to the extract source for full bibliographical information about any of these.

Author

Judith Roden is a Principal Lecturer in the Faculty of Education at Canterbury Christ Church University. She is currently the primary science team leader, has had several articles published and is co-author of *Teaching Science in the Primary Classroom: a practical guide* (Paul Chapman).

Series editor

Professor Sonia Blandford is Pro-Vice Chancellor (Dean of Education) at Canterbury Christ Church University, one of the largest providers of initial teacher training and professional development in the United Kingdom. Following a successful career as a teacher in primary and secondary schools, Sonia has worked in higher education for nine years. She has acted as an education consultant to ministries of education in Eastern Europe, South America and South Africa and as an adviser to the European Commission, LEAs and schools. She co-leads the Teach First initiative. The author of a range of education management texts, she has a reputation for her straightforward approach to difficult issues. Her publications include: *Middle Management in*

Schools (Pearson), *Resource Management in Schools* (Pearson), *Professional Development Manual* (Pearson), *School Discipline Manual* (Pearson), *Managing Special Educational Needs in Schools* (Sage), *Managing Discipline in Schools* (Routledge), *Managing Professional Development in Schools* (Routledge), *Financial Management in Schools* (Optimus), *Remodelling Schools: Workforce Reform* (Pearson) and *Sonia Blandford's Masterclass* (Sage).

Acknowledgements

Every effort has been made to trace the copyright holders and to obtain their permission for the use of copyright material. The publisher and author will gladly receive information enabling them to rectify any error or omission in subsequent editions.

The author and publisher would like to thank the following for permission to reproduce copyright material:

Asoko, H 'Developing conceptual understanding in primary science', *Cambridge Journal of Education*, vol 32, no. 2, 2002. Reproduced with kind permission of Taylor & Francis Ltd. http://www.tandf.co.uk/journals; Duggan, S and Gott, R 'What sort of science education do we really need?' *International Journal of Science Education*, vol. 24, no. 7, 2002. Reproduced with kind permission of Taylor & Francis Ltd. http://www.tandf.co.uk/journals; Harlen, W and Winter, J 'The development of assessment for learning: learning from the case of science and mathematics'. *Language Testing*, vol. 21, no. 3, 2004. Reproduced with kind permission of Hodder Arnold Journals; Harlen W and Qualter, A *The teaching of science in primary schools*, David Fulton 2004. Reproduced with kind permission of David Fulton Publishers www.fultonpublishers.co.uk; Mercer, N, Dawes, L, Wegerif, R and Sams C, 'Reasoning as a scientist: ways of helping children to use language to learn science', *British Educational Research Journal*, vol. 30, no. 3, June 2000. Reproduced with kind permission of Taylor & Francis Ltd. http://www.tandf.co.uk/journals; NACCCE/DfEE *All our future: creativity, culture and educations*, DfEE 1999. Reproduced with kind permission of DfEE; Newton, P D and Newton, L D 'Do teachers support casual understanding through their discourse when teaching primary science?' *British Educational Research Journal*, vol. 26, no. 5, 2000. Reproduced with kind permission of Taylor & Francis Ltd. http://www.tandf.co.uk/journals; Ovens P, 'A "SANE" way to encourage creativity', *Primary Science Review*, 81, Jan/Feb 2004. Reproduced with kind permission of Peter Ovens; QCA, *Assessing progress in science teachers' guide*, QCA. Reproduced with kind permission of QCA (Enterprises) Ltd; QCA, *National Curriculum Tests 2004: Implications for teaching and learning from the 2004 tests*, QCA. Reproduced with kind permission of QCA (Enterprises) Ltd; QCA, *Science Key Stage 2 2001 Test B level 3-5, Science Key Stage 2 2002 Test A level 3-5, Science Key Stage 2 2003 Test B level 3-5, Science Key Stage 2 2004 Test B level 3-5, Science Key Stage 2 2005 Test A level 3-5*, QCA. Reproduced with kind permission of QCA (Enterprises) Ltd; Qualter, A, *Differentiated primary science*, Open University Press, 1966; Robinson, W P 'Single-sex teaching and achievement in science', *International Journal of Science Education*, 14 May 2004, vol. 26, no. 6, Routledge. Reproduced with kind permission of Taylor & Francis Ltd. http://www.tandf.co.uk/journals;

Rutledge, N 'Genesis of the ice trolls', *Primary Science Review*, 81, Jan/Feb 2004, The Association for Science Education; Sears, J and Sorensen, P *Issues in Science Education*, RoutledgeFalmer 2000. Reproduced with kind permission of Taylor & Francis Ltd. http://www.tandf.co.uk/journals; Sherrington, R (ed.), *ASE guide to primary science education*, Hatfield ASE/StanleyThornes 1988. Reproduced with kind permission of Hatfield ASE/StanleyThornes; Sturman, L 'Teaching to the test: science or intuition', *Educational Research*, vol. 45, no. 3, Winter, Routledge. Reproduced with kind permission of Taylor & Francis Ltd. http://www.tandf.co.uk/journals; Topping, K, Peter, C, Stephen, P and Whele, M, 'Cross-age peer tutoring of science in the primary school: influence on scientific language and thinking', *Educational Psychology*, vol. 24, no. 1, Feb 2004, Carfax. Reproduced with kind permission of Taylor & Francis Ltd. http://www.tandf.co.uk/journals; Torrance, H and Pryor, J 'Developing formative assessment in the classroom: using action research to explore and modify theory', *British Educational Research Journal*, Carfax. Reproduced with kind permission of Taylor & Francis Ltd. http://www.tandf.co.uk/journals; Van Praagh, G (ed.), *H E Armstrong and scientific education*, John Murray 1973; Ward, H, Roden, J, Hewlett, C and Foreman, J, *Teaching science in the primary classroom: a practical guide*, Paul Chapman Publishing 2005. Reproduced with kind permission of Sage Publications Ltd; Wellington, J *Practical work in school science: which way now?* Routledge 1998. Reproduced with kind permission of Taylor & Francis Ltd. http://www.tandf.co.uk/journals; Wenham, M *Understanding primary science: ideas, concepts and explanations*, Sage Publications 2005. Reproduced with kind permission of Sage Publications Ltd.

1 Science and school science

By the end of this chapter you should have:

- considered **why** it is important for all pupils to study science for the benefit of the individual and society;
- reflected on **what** it means to be scientific and the nature of scientific understanding;
- analysed **how** science can contribute to a person's general education and how the previously portrayed view of science can be translated into teaching science in the primary classroom.

Linking your learning

Sharp, J, Peacock, G, Johnsey, R, Simon, S, and Smith, R (2002) *Achieving QTS. Primary science: teaching theory and practice.* Chapter 2. Exeter: Learning Matters.

Professional Standards for QTS
1.7, 2.1a, 2.1b, 2.4

Introduction

This chapter will explore the nature of scientific understanding and the implications for science in the primary school. As Sharp *et al.* (2002) tell us, while not everyone will become a professional scientist, those people who use scientific methods in their approach to life and its problems are more likely to have a realistic understanding, than those who depend on hearsay or make inaccurate observations and poor interpretations. This chapter will encourage you to think of science as a fundamental, worthwhile aspect of primary education. The aim of science in the primary school and beyond is to provide children with opportunities to develop their awareness and understanding of science alongside their ability to work in a scientific way.

A common personal response to science is that it is a cold, objective subject full of absolute truths and that science education consists of facts to be learned. In reality, science is more about looking at the world, weighing up evidence objectively and being prepared to change understanding. The aim of science education is, first, to provide children with knowledge and understanding and, second, to provide the skills to meet a fast-changing future with the confidence and ability to make decisions about scientific issues in the increasingly technological world. The aim, therefore, is to make every individual scientifically literate.

Why?

Why is it important for all children to study science for the benefit of the individual and society?

Before you read the following extract, take a few minutes to reflect and note down your response to the following:

- What is your understanding of the nature of science? What does 'science' mean to you?
- What is your own experience of school science?
- What is your current attitude towards science and things scientific?
- Then draw a scientist.

Extract: Harlen, W and Qualter, A (2004) 'The goals of learning science', chapter 6 in *The teaching of science in primary schools*, **London: David Fulton.**

Scientific literacy: an overall aim
Scientific literacy is the term used for the essential understanding that should be part of everyone's education. Just as the term 'literacy' on its own denotes competence in using language at the level needed for functioning effectively in society, so scientific literacy indicates a competence in relation to science:

- being able to function with confidence in relation to the scientific aspects of the world around;
- being able to look at something 'in a scientific way', seeing for example, whether or not evidence has been taken into account in the explanation of an event or phenomenon, whether it makes sense in terms of related events or phenomena, and so on;
- being aware of the nature of (and limitations of) scientific knowledge and the role of values in its generation.

The term 'scientific literacy' is used in statements about the aims of science education in various countries and in statements of international bodies such as UNESCO and the OECD. The definition used in the OECD Programme for International Student Achievement (PISA) is as follows:

> The capacity to use scientific knowledge to identify questions and to draw evidence-based conclusions in order to understand and help make decisions about the natural world and the changes made to it through human activity (OECD 2003, p.133).

In the UK, an influential report (*Beyond 2000: Science Education for the Future*) recommended that *the science curriculum for 5-16 should be seen primarily as a course to enhance general scientific literacy* (Millar and Osborne, 1998, p9). What this means is explained below.

The science curriculum should:

- sustain and develop the curiosity of young people about the natural world around them, and build up their confidence in their ability to enquire into its behaviour. It should seek to foster a sense of wonder, enthusiasm and interest in science so that young people feel confident and competent to engage with scientific and technical matters;
- help young people acquire a broad, general understanding of the important ideas and explanatory frameworks of science, and of the procedures of scientific enquiry, which have had a major impact on our material environment and on our culture in general, so that they can:

  - appreciate why these ideas are valued;
  - appreciate the underlying rationale for decisions (for example, about diet, or medical treatment, or energy use) which they may wish or be advised to take in everyday contexts, both now and in later life;
  - be able to understand, and respond critically to, media reports of issues with a science component;
  - feel empowered to hold and express a personal point of view on issues with a science component which enter the arena of public debate and perhaps to become actively involved in some of these;
  - acquire further knowledge, when required, either for interest or for vocational purposes.

The contribution of primary science to scientific literacy

The aims of developing scientific literacy, as described here may seem remote from primary science, but they are in essence easily identified as developing attitudes ('a sense of wonder, enthusiasm and interest'), developing ideas ('understanding of important ideas and explanatory frameworks') and developing process skills ('the procedures for scientific enquiry'). Primary science has a contribution to make to all of these. We just have to remember that in all cases we are talking about development, starting from the simple foundations that are needed for more abstract ideas and advanced thinking.

Analysis

Harlen and Qualter put forward a convincing argument for all future citizens to be scientifically literate. At first glance, it might seem difficult to see what sort of experiences need to be provided at the primary stage to lay the foundations for developing the kind of knowledge, skills, and pertinently, the awareness of science and the issues surrounding it in the modern world. Given the rapid developments in science and technology it is likely that future citizens will need a working knowledge of science that is far different from that provided in traditional education. What this actually means for your own practice in the primary classroom will be considered later, but you will need to reflect on and to be open-minded about what should count as primary science education in the twenty-first century, and what primary pupils need to 'know' and what form this knowledge should take.

Although Harlen is very clear in her view of scientific literacy, it seems that there is no universal understanding of the term. After a review of literature, Murphy *et al.* (2001, p190) suggest that there is not one accepted definition. In the UK, it is generally known as 'public understanding of science'. They cite Bybee's (1997) view that scientific literacy is best defined as *a continuum of understanding about the natural and designed world* and that *as a metaphor, the term 'scientific literacy' refers to being well-educated and well informed in science.* Murphy *et al.* also point out that it can merely mean understanding scientific vocabulary. Clearly this is a far cry from Harlen's more inclusive vision of scientific literacy, where there is a marrying of knowledge and understanding with process skills and attitudes which act together over time to produce the scientifically literate adult.

It can be argued that, given the limited science background of many citizens in the UK, there is a need to raise awareness about the major science-related issues facing modern society. Significantly, in the run-up to the general election in May 2005, there were a number of issues explored in the media relating to employment and the nature and needs of society as a whole. One such issue related to immigration, including illegal immigration and the debates about particular skills shortages and employment issues. The second related to the ceasing of car production at Rover in Birmingham that cost over 4000 manufacturing jobs in the car industry, symptomatic of the trend away from traditional manufacturing in Britain while it is increasing in other parts of the world, noticeably in the Far East. The car industry is typical of many manufacturing industries that have hi-tech origins where scientific knowledge has been applied and technological development has been the result. The argument is very relevant to the current state of the nation, its immediate future and the future of science education. At the same time, politicians were very quiet about long-term significant issues, such as energy generation.

Some of the issues, notable by their absence in the debate, tend to be science related and be long term. Such issues typically require citizens to have a certain level of scientific literacy and understanding of the issues; for example, those that relate to nuclear power and wind generation. Both can provoke much emotional subjective responses that are often aggravated by coverage in the media.

It is important for you to consider to what extent you believe yourself to be scientifically literate in Harlen's terms and to identify what factors in your own education contributed to your personal level of scientific literacy.

Personal response

Look back at your response to the pre-reading task.

To what extent do you believe that your own school education in science fostered in you a sense of wonder, enthusiasm and interest in science?

As a result of your own science education do you feel confident and competent to engage with scientific and technical matters?

To what extent do you consider yourself to be 'scientifically literate'?

Practical implications and activities

- What experiences in your own science education do you think contributed to your own level of scientific literacy?
- What were the positive factors involved?
- What were the factors that worked against the intended outcome?
- Identify and record your own strengths and areas for development in this area.

Current issues of science in society

Discuss with a colleague your immediate reaction to the following proposals to meet the increasing demand for electricity in the UK:

- the commissioning of a number of nuclear power stations;
- the development of pockets of wind turbines across the UK.

Make a note of all the arguments you can think of, both for and against these proposals.

Identify the origin of your views.

Further reading

Hoyle, P and Stane, C (2000) 'Developing the literate scientist', in Sears, J and Sorensen, P, *Issues in science education.* London: RoutledgeFalmer.

What?

What does it mean to be scientific and what is the nature of scientific understanding?

Before you read the following extract, read:

- Harlen, W (2000) 'The goals of science education', in *Teaching, learning and assessing science 5–12*, 3rd edn. London: Paul Chapman Publishing.
- Ratcliffe, M (1998) 'The purposes of science education', in Sherrington, R (ed) *ASE guide to primary science education.* Hatfield: ASE/Stanley Thornes.

Extract: Roden, J and Ward, H (2005) 'What is science?', chapter 1, in Ward, H et al. Teaching science in the primary classroom: A practical guide. London: Sage Publications Ltd.

The four threads of science
Historically, science has had two aspects: first, a body of knowledge and, second, a way of working. The two aspects are totally and inextricably linked. Whenever scientists work, they find out about the world using aspects of scientific method. Similarly, pre-school children find out about the world using the same basic methods. Although the level of sophistication and the tools used in their tasks will be different, both scientists and pupils find out about the world using the same processes. For many years, in theory, if not always in popular practice, one of the principle aims of science education

has been to develop pupils' understanding through the use of scientific approaches. Being scientific also involves the development of concepts like electricity or change or movement, etc. There is a strong relationship between pupils' use of scientific method and the development of scientific understanding. Furthermore, developments in both aspects of science are strongly influenced by, and rely upon, scientists and pupils' attitudes towards science. The attitudes involved in 'being scientific', generally includes curiosity, respect for evidence, willingness to tolerate uncertainty, creativity and inventiveness, open-mindedness, critical reflection, co-operation with others, sensitivity to living and non-living things and perseverance. Although Johnson (1996) sees scientific development as a 'triple helix' with three threads, conceptual understanding, skills and attitudes all developing together to support later understanding, a further area is important in joining the strands together and this is the area of scientific procedures. Scientific procedures are different from skills and include the nature of science and the development of scientific ideas. These four threads are linked and are vital if science is to continue to have any relevance for the pupils in the twenty-first century. For without this breadth, science is a dry and limiting subject which fails to interest and excite, where the past trials and successes are reduced to a list of facts to be learnt and experiments to be conducted.

The importance of group work

Unlike many subjects of the primary curriculum, science provides the opportunity for working as a group rather than working independently within a group situation. Science enables pupils to be involved in group work where they have the opportunity to share ideas and co-operate with each other in collaborative practical activity. Research shows that pupils who work together learn more than when working alone. Sharing ideas and group work are also important to scientific activity. When asked what qualities were needed to solve a scientific problem, an eminent scientist replied:

> The ability to ask the right question is very important … perseverance and determination … Lateral thinking is useful when a straightforward solution to the problem is not obvious. The ability to admit that the scientific evidence shows that your pet idea is wrong and someone else's idea is right is also important. Today, much science is done in teams, so the ability to work in a team is helpful. (**www.acclaimscientists.org.uk**).

Clearly these qualities are not exclusive to science and scientists and therefore the development of these qualities should be at the heart of education. However, being able to work as part of a group is needed if pupils' procedural understanding and scientific attitudes are to be developed. Practical science provides many opportunities not only for the sharing and challenging of ideas amongst peers, but also for the development of group skills. The role of the teacher is crucial in this process:

> neglect of the process skills means that children have to take ideas as given by teacher or text book and there is a great deal of experience that shows that this is unlikely to lead to understanding (Sherrington, 1998, p28).

If the teacher always plans the investigation, providing only opportunities for illustrative activities, i.e. those that illustrate a concept or scientific principle, the skill of planning will be lost. Starting with the pupils' own ideas is important, as they need to develop their ideas progressively in a variety of topics throughout their primary years. Pupils need to be taught how to ask questions and find the answers using a wide range of approaches and, in doing so, to collect evidence. Approaching collected data with an open mind, trying to make sense of any developing patterns and drawing conclusions are activities that develop respect for evidence. Collaborative group work introduces pupils to the social aspects of science as well as providing opportunities for the development of key learning skills. All these features are interwoven and support the development of pupil attitudes towards science, which have a major impact on learning.

The nature of scientific ideas
The amount of scientific knowledge and understanding is immense and has been developed over thousands of years. Some original ideas have been challenged over time, for example, that the earth is the centre of the universe and flat. Other ideas have been refined over time, for example, the idea that the atom is composed of neutrons, electrons and protons. However, most of the ideas in science accepted as true today have one thing in common: that there is some evidence to support them. Conclusions have been drawn and have been communicated to others, which has resulted in the ideas being challenged and rejected or accepted. Pupils should develop an understanding of the ways in which facts have changed over time, and this aspect of science should be included in the teaching and learning approaches used in the primary school. If it is not, then science merely becomes a body of knowledge that has to be learnt, with no opportunities for a new slant or a creative response on behalf of the pupils. The focus on what is known rather than how it is known makes science sterile. Evaluating evidence is important in science and is also an important generic life skill. Open-mindedness and respect for evidence are important attitudes in science and important also to everyday life, i.e. making decisions based on evidence rather than jumping to conclusions.

Analysis

So what is the nature of science and scientific understanding? Roden and Ward (2005) explore the nature of science and consider the implication for the education of young people. Developing the theme, it is clear that for both children and scientists, as Sharp *et al.* (2002) say, the nature of scientific understanding is built up over long periods of time:

- scientific understanding is based on previously accumulated knowledge which may be expressed in terms of generalisations;
- the more evidence that supports an idea, the more we might accept it as valid;
- scientific ideas are often tentative;
- a successful theory will enable successful predictions to be made;
- the quality of the scientific knowledge and understanding is dependent on the quality of the scientific skills used to gather evidence and interpret it (p7–8).

Ratcliffe (1998, p5) makes it clear that every teacher needs to explore the philosophy of science to ensure that they can articulate a clear perspective of their own. Too often, she says, because we lack an exploration of the nature of science in our own education, our views on the nature of science, and therefore its translation into school science, are underdeveloped. She makes the point forcefully that values are being transmitted in every science classroom either implicitly or explicitly. Therefore, it is important for you to explore these aspects for yourself. Your own understanding of the nature and philosophy of science should ensure that you are providing children with a view of science that is a creative, human endeavour influenced by cultures and beliefs rather than, as Ratcliffe suggests, a collection of objective, value-free facts. The worry is of course that for many years, unintentionally perhaps, the latter has dominated popular science education. You will need to ensure that you avoid conveying an inappropriate message about science.

Science is an important part of the primary curriculum. The approach needed to promote the well-used aim of science education, i.e. to *develop an enquiring mind and a scientific approach to solving problems* is one that, as Harlen puts it in the first extract, *should seek to foster a sense of wonder, enthusiasm and interest in science so that young people feel confident and competent to engage with scientific and technical matters.* Here, you need to consider your own attitude towards science; your own understanding of the nature of science and the factors that have influenced you can significantly influence the way you teach science in your classroom. Many teachers' attitudes towards science and teaching science have been coloured by their own, often unsuccessful, experience in their own education. Traditional strategies that largely excluded a stimulating, practical, problem-solving approach have done little to enthuse and communicate the potentially exciting science that is relevant to children today. You need to be a good role model and construct well-planned, relevant activities that provide opportunities for your children to become enthusiastic young scientists.

Science is both a body of knowledge and a way of working. It should be everyone's entitlement to receive a wide-ranging basis of science, including exploration of the nature of science at all levels of education, in order to equip individuals for a greater understanding of the nature of science in modern society.

Personal response

Look back to your initial response to the pre-reading task on page 8:

- Explore your own experiences of science education.
- To what extent were opportunities provided to develop your understanding of the whole of 'science' including the nature of science?
- What sorts of activities were provided?
- What was your attitude towards science at school?
- What factors influenced your attitudes?
- Having reflected on the nature of science and on your own experience of science education, what implications are there for your own teaching of science in school? Make a note of these for later reference.
- What does science contribute to a child's whole education that is not provided in any other subject area?

Practical implications and activities

With a colleague or peer, analyse your personal responses and highlight the similarities and differences.

Look at your drawing of a scientist. Ask a few children to undertake a similar drawing. What does this indicate about images of scientists? Where have these ideas come from?

Search the internet for pictures of scientists. What conclusions do you reach about how science is portrayed?

Look at the role of girls in children's TV programmes such as *Scooby Doo* and *Dexter's Laboratory*. What image do these provide of girls and science?

It is often thought that science is an objective activity lacking in any moral responsibility. This view is often reinforced and compounded by the way that scientific developments are reported in the media. In one newspaper in April 2005, there were two separate articles reporting on the following:

The first was entitled: 'Sex selection. Cloning. "Right to die". Slowly, human existence is being reduced to a mere bundle of cells to be grown, manipulated or destroyed at will'. *Daily Mail*, Wednesday, 30 March.

The article commented on a court ruling concerning the tubes delivering water and food to a woman who had been in a persistent vegetative state for 15 years. The court decided that it was in the best interests of the patient to remove the tubes.

The second described a man, in Australia, reporting a crime in a British town that he witnessed as it was filmed by CCTV and transmitted on the internet.

This incident highlights the almost unbelievable ways in which science and technology have contributed to change.

What was your reaction to these articles? What factors influenced your views?

Identify a recent scientific 'happening' in the media. To what extent did you understand the argument presented? Did the article present a number of opinions and attitudes, or did you detect any evidence of bias? What was your attitude towards the event? What principle underpins your reaction to this event?

Now, with your colleague, choose a current science related issue of interest to you and search for information about it on the internet. Weigh up the evidence. Do your findings reflect the way the issue is reported in the media?

Further reading

Dawson, C (2000) 'Upper primary boys' and girls' interest in science: have they changed since 1980?', *International Journal of Science Education,* 22 (6) 557–570.

Jarvis, T and Pell, A (2002) 'Changes in primary boys' and girls' attitudes to school and science during a two-year science in-service programme', *The Curriculum Journal* 13 (1) Spring 43-69.

How?

How can science contribute to a person's general education, and how can the previously portrayed view of science be translated into teaching science in the primary classroom?

Before you read the following extract, read:

- Ratcliffe, M (2004) 'The nature of science' in Sharp, J (ed) *Developing primary science*. Exeter: Learning Matters.

Extract: Ratcliffe, M (1998) 'The purposes of science education', chapter 1.1 in Sherrington, R (ed.) *ASE Guide to Primary Science Education*. Hatfield: ASE/Stanley Thornes.

Purposes of science education
To gain an appreciation of the underlying purposes of the science National Curriculum, we could again refer to the non-statutory guidance. This offers the following as the contributions of science to the school curriculum:

1. Understanding the key concepts of science will allow pupils to use them in unfamiliar situations.
2. Using scientific methods of investigation will help pupils to make successful, disciplined enquiries and use ideas to solve relevant problems.
3. Appreciating the contributions science makes to society will encourage pupils to develop a sense of their responsibilities as members of society and the contributions they can make to it.
4. Learning in science contributes to personal development.
5. Appreciating the powerful but provisional nature of scientific knowledge and explanation will bring pupils closer to the process by which scientific models are created, tested and modified.
6. Giving students access to careers in science and design and technology is vital.
(NCC, 1989, pA4)

In looking to the future, Scottish CCC suggests that, for individual learners, experience of science education should:

- broaden understanding of themselves, human culture and societies and the natural and made worlds in which they live;
- help to sustain natural human curiosity, develop an enquiring mind and foster an interest in continuing to learn throughout life;
- help to engender a critical way of thinking about phenomena and issues;
- support other aspects of learning across the curriculum;

- develop the potential to contribute in an informed thoughtful and sensitive way to the enhancement of people's lives and of the environment. (Scottish CCC, 1996)

The science national curriculum in Northern Ireland has the following in the introduction to the Programme of Study at Key Stage 3:

> Pupils should consider the benefits and drawbacks of applying scientific and technological ideas to themselves, industry, the environment and the community. They should begin to make personal decisions and judgements based on their scientific knowledge of issues concerning personal health and well being, safety and the care of the environment. Through this study, pupils should begin to develop an understanding of how science shapes and influences the quality of their lives.

All three of these descriptions bring in their respective underlying views of science and, importantly, the personal development of the pupil.

Some science educators have argued for science education as a grounding in 'scientific literacy' or for the 'public understanding of science'. The UK Curriculum Council's descriptions of pupils' experiences have some similarity to the three strands of scientific literacy agreed by the many commentators (e.g. AAS, 1989; Driver et al., 1996; Millar, 1996). Pupils should gain:

- knowledge and understanding of some science concepts;
- an understanding that scientific endeavours are social human activities, involving value judgements and cultural contexts;
- an understanding of the processes involved in the conduct of and reasoning about science.

However, we still have to answer the question, Why do we consider these strands so important in pupils' education? Millar (1996) groups the arguments for 'public understanding of science' into five categories:

1. Economic – there is a connection between the level of public understanding of science and the nation's wealth.
2. Utility – an understanding of science is useful practically in a technological society.
3. Democratic – an understanding of science is necessary to partcipate in decision making about issues with a base in science.
4. Social – it is important to maintain links between science and the wider culture.
5. Cultural – science is the major achievement of our culture and all young people should be enabled to understand and appreciate it.

No simple slogan – 'scientific literacy', 'public understanding of science', 'citizen science' – can adequately convey how these strands interrelate. Figure 1.1a is one attempt to portray the elements contributing to scientific literacy.

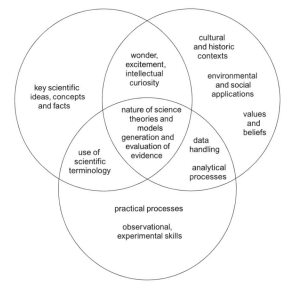

Figure 1.1a Elements of science

This alone cannot constitute an adequate description of the purposes of science education. The development of the individual pupil is important. Figure 1.1b shows how the elements of 'scientific literacy' could contribute to pupils' personal development.

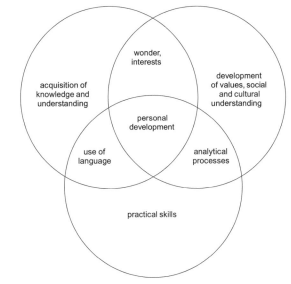

Figure 1.1b Education of the whole person

If any one of the areas in Figures1.1a and 1.1b is missing, then the individual's education is impoverished. Equally, pupils can miss out if the purposes are skewed in any way through particular methods of curriculum interpretation. This can happen, for example, if the acquisition of facts and concepts is emphasised at the expense of development of analytical skills.

Analysis

Ratcliffe (2004) provides a comprehensive exploration of the nature and different perceptions of science, explores what children understand about the nature of science, and considers what this topic should cover. This is important at all levels of science education. In the extract, she provides an excellent summary of the reasons for the importance of science both to the individual and to society. This is pertinent to our examination of primary science today and in the future.

Looking back to the National Curriculum Non-Statutory Guidance (NCC, 1989) provides an insight into the thinking behind the very first National Curriculum Statutory Orders (DES, 1989) and the intentions for practice. This document was published to provide guidance on 'why' and 'how' the new curriculum should be put into practice, because while the science National Curriculum stated what should be taught and what would be assessed at each key stage, it failed to provide guidance on how this should be implemented. Although science was a core subject under the 1988 Education Reform Act (DES, 1988), most teachers had little experience of teaching science, with little or no training; many had a reluctance to do so and few had a strong background in science. Nevertheless, the National Curriculum appreciated that the contribution of science to society was important, as was an understanding of the nature of science, and also that providing access to science-related careers was crucial (NCC, 1989).

Given the hurdles facing the implementation of the science National Curriculum in 1989, it is amazing that so much has been achieved to date (Parliamentary Office for Science and Technology, 2003), but the primary science curriculum is still evolving. Two revisions later, it is pertinent to look to the future as the Scottish CCC did in 1996. Interestingly, their proposals match today's vision for the future outlined in the current government's Green Paper, *Every Child Matters* (DfES 2003) and the challenges for the futures agenda (**http://itefutures.tta.gov.uk**).

Everyone should understand the contribution science can make to the individual and to society, yet many do not, including many politicians and other influential people whose background is not likely to be science-based. Consequently there is a potential danger that individuals may not benefit from the higher level generic skills that science can provide the opportunity to develop in order to compete in today's global markets. There is a need to highlight the potential contribution of science in society since there is much public ignorance. This may have implications for the way science is delivered in the classroom. Crucially, you and other practitioners must recognise and implement the 'right kind of science education', to examine and reflect on your own practice and that of others and to facilitate the kind of science advocated by the science community.

Personal response

Thinking about the potential of science education and your own teaching experience, what do you think science can offer to the education of the whole child?

To what extent do you think primary education contributes to the development of the scientifically literate population?

Practical implications and activities

Look back at Figures 1.1a and 1.1b in the Ratcliffe extract. Match the elements of science with your own or observed practice.

- Which aspects are catered for?
- Which aspects are not?
- How does your own science teaching contribute to each identified aspect of the whole person?

What are the implications for your practice?

Think about the five outcomes set out in the Green Paper (DfES, 2003), i.e. the need for each child to:
- be healthy;
- stay safe;
- enjoy achieving;
- make a positive contribution;
- achieve economic well-being.

Talk to a colleague. Where does science fit in here? How will your work in science help children achieve these aims for the future?

Think about your teaching of science in the future. Make a note of how you think it might change to meet the needs of the individual and the changing society in which we live.

Further reading

Bricheno, P, Johnson, J and Sears, J (2000) 'Children's attitudes towards science: beyond the men in white coats', in Sears, J and Sorensen, P. *Issues in science education*. London: RoutledgeFalmer.

2 Science as a creative activity

By the end of this chapter you should have:

- considered **why** science should be seen as a creative activity;
- reflected upon **what** creative science should look like;
- analysed **how** creativity can be recognised in the learner.

Linking your learning

Sharp, J, Peacock, G, Johnsey, R, Simon, S, and Smith, R (2002) *Achieving QTS. Primary science: teaching theory and practice,* Chapter 2. Exeter: Learning Matters.

Professional Standards for QTS
1.7, 2.1a, 2.1b, 2.4, 3.1.1, 3.1.3

Introduction

Many scientists claim that science is a creative activity. This view is frequently not shared by non-scientists who often perceive science to be a convergent not a divergent activity. This suggests that there is a general misunderstanding of science in the wider community: scientists have failed to communicate the real nature of their art. There may well be many reasons for this. It could be that many people do not really understand the fundamental nature of science, not least because of the way that science has been taught at many levels in the past. The stark differences between these views of the nature of science have led to recent discussions about how the science curriculum should change to reflect the more creative divergent nature of science.

Undoubtedly, as the National Advisory Committee on Creative and Cultural Education (NACCCE, 1999, p27) remind us, the term 'creativity' has a particular association with the arts, whereas science tends to be thought of as uncreative. Why is this the case? Possibly it is because people find it difficult to conceptualise science as creative. Certainly, explicit mention of science is conspicuous by its absence in the highly influential DfES (2003) document *Excellence and Enjoyment*. At the other end of the spectrum, the location of science in the Foundation Stage 'Knowledge and Understanding of the World' separated from subjects classed as 'creative' does not help. Added to this, the perception of science as an 'objective', cold subject may well have been reinforced as a result of the artificial separation of science from technology in the National Curriculum proposals in 1988. Creativity may well be more easily recognised in design technology than in science, but there is a close relationship between science and technology and this needs to be understood. First though, it is necessary to examine and understand the claims of science as a creative activity. Your own perception of science may well make this hard to believe. You may well be questioning whether science can truly be seen as a creative activity.

Why?

Why should science be seen as a creative activity?

Before you read the following extract, read:

- NACCCE (1999) 'Creative education', in *All our futures: creativity, culture and education.* London: DfEE.
- Standler, R B (1998) Creativity in science and engineering. **www.rbs0.com/ create.htm**

Extract: NACCCE (1999) *All our futures: creativity, culture and education*, **pp31–33. London: DfEE.**

The processes of creativity

Creative abilities are developed through practical application: by being engaged in the processes of creative thought production: making music, writing stories, conducting experiments, and so on. A key task for teachers is to help young people to understand these processes and to gain control of them. These are particular techniques and skills which are specific to different disciplines and forms of work. But there are some general features of creative processes which young people need to experience and recognise.

Creative processes in all disciplines usually involve an initial phase of drafting: of giving an idea a rough shape or outline. The process of development is commonly one of 'successive approximations' in which the idea is shaped and clarified in the process of exploring it. The final phases are often to do with refining the detail of expression … The classical division of stages in creative thought – preparation-incubation-illumination then verification … Creative activity involves a complex combination of controlled and non-controlled elements, unconscious as well as conscious mental processes, non-directed as well as directed thought, intuitive as well as rational calculation.

At the right time and in the right way, rigorous critical appraisal is essential. At the wrong point, criticism and the cold hand of realism can kill an emerging idea.

We said earlier that creativity is possible in all areas of human activity and not only in the arts. This is clearly true. Creative insights and advances have driven forward human culture in the sciences, in technology, in philosophy, the arts and the humanities. The history of science, indeed, the essential process is one of continuous conjectures and of re-evaluations of established ideas: of new insights or information, challenging and building on existing knowledge. This is the source of the intellectual excitement and creative impulse of science: it is concerned not only with facts but with what counts as facts, and not just with observation but with explanation, interpretation and meaning. The processes of scientific analysis and investigation can involve the highest levels of creativity and insight. Discovery in science is not always strictly logical. It often results from unexpected leaps of imagination: from sudden moments of illumination in which

---

the scientist grasps the answer to a question and sets out to verify it by calculation. This can be as true for children setting out as for experienced scientists.

Leap of the imagination

Some of the most common science activities can provide opportunities for teachers to witness a creative leap of the imagination where children suddenly make a connection and move their own learning forward. Children were testing different materials to find out which one was waterproof. They used a range of materials, looked at them under a microscope and made the connection that those materials with holes allowed water to flow through and that the bigger the hole, the faster the water flowed through the material. Whilst most children accepted that some fabrics were waterproof and some others were not, one child, silent for a while, obviously pondering on the different aspects of the activity, suddenly exclaimed, 'We need to fill the holes to make it waterproof. If we crayoned over the fabric the wax would go into the holes.' This illustrates where a child does not take the obvious route and also shows real understanding of the key idea.

Analysis

Why *should* science be seen as a creative subject? On first reading, the extract appears not to answer the question. However, if we examine the ideas and motives that under-pin the move towards creativity in education, we may well be able to see the relevance. Essentially, the extract encapsulates the nature of science and the main points of science as a creative endeavour. It does not though, explore 'why' it is impor-tant for everyone to see science in this way. It would be easy to accept the move towards seeing creativity in science as expressed in the DfES (2003) document *Excellence and Enjoyment* without critical examination of the thinking underpinning the approach. It is, however, important to question and to understand the reasons put forward for this move.

Essentially, the UK needs more scientists and, ideally, creative scientists. The education system needs to produce future creative scientists who can expand the current bound-aries of science and technology. Examples of such creativity in science from the past are readily available. Archimedes and displacement, Newton and gravity, Priestley and the discovery of oxygen, Marie Curie and radium, Fleming and penicillin, Darwin and natural selection – we could easily add more. Frequently developments come about by accident, when scientists are researching something else, e.g. Viagra is now used as a treatment for male sexual dysfunction after unexpected observations when it was being trialled as a treatment for heart attacks. Importantly, education needs not only to produce the creative ideas that will bring economic success in the future, but also to encourage children to adopt science at an early stage of education.

Recently, there has been emphasis placed on the individual in society, made explicit in the Green Paper *Every Child Matters* (DfES, 2003), underlining the need for indivi-duals to be healthy and to be safe. The development of medicines and safe products is fundamental and critical if this objective is to be achieved. With this in mind it is criti-cal that enough scientists are produced to meet the demands of our highly developed technological society. New threats to the health of the population such as MRSA and 'bird flu' urgently need to be researched and solutions found to these and other potential health problems.

All this highlights the important role of the primary teacher in the future. More children must develop positive attitudes towards science at the primary stage, but how best can this be achieved? You will need not only to provide opportunities for creativity in science, but also to recognise when children are being creative. The extract above provides a starting point for understanding. Here children are raising new ideas and are exhibiting creative thought. It needs to be recognised that children do not necessarily need to suggest a totally new idea, rather, the idea may be new to that child or group of children.

Personal response

Many people do not consider science to be interesting and creative and do not see the relevance of science in their own lives. Such individuals consider that there is no need for them to hold any knowledge and understanding of science. Worryingly, many of these adults are also parents who could influence young people who are choosing the direction of their future.

Where do you stand on this issue?

Why do you think it is important for the future to promote science as a creative activity?

Practical implications and activities

Task 1

Standler (1998) explores the nature of creativity in science and engineering. He provides very interesting insights into the characteristics of the creative scientist. In particular, he provides the following definition of creativity:

> A creative person does things that have never been done before. Particularly important instances for creativity include discoveries of new knowledge in science and medicine, invention of new technology, composing beautiful music, or analysing a situation (e.g. in law, philosophy, or history) in a new way.

He believes that it is important to distinguish between intelligence, creativity and academic qualifications, i.e. that those who develop significant ideas are intelligent, highly qualified people but often not creative, and students who are both intelligent and highly creative often do not perform exceptionally well in school.

What do you think of this viewpoint?

- Compare and contrast the NACCCE's view of creativity with that of Standler. Which do you find most relevant?

- With a colleague, think about aspects of your own life when you have been creative. Where were you and what were you doing when you were being creative in the wider sense of the word?
- Identify the factors/influences that contributed to this.

Can you find examples in your own experience to support or deny this point?

Task 2

Standler (1998) also claims that the ability to think creatively is the amalgamation of several different kinds of intelligence and personality traits. Among the personality traits he identifies, those linked with creative output are:

- diligence;
- stubbornness;
- eccentricity;
- reclusiveness, since most landmark discoveries in science are the work of one person.

If Standler is correct, this holds implications not only for science teaching, but also for how we view individual responses in science in the classroom.

- Think about these ideas in relation to your teaching.
- What are the implications for practical work?
- Can any of these traits be identified in your children?

How does this impact on group work in science?

Further reading

Head, J (1985) 'Towards a psychology of science', in *The personal response to science*. Cambridge University Press. In chapter 1, Head considers the objectivity of science and provides evidence to suggest that even the most important work in science is coloured by subjectivity.

What?

What does creative science look like?

Before you read the following extract, note examples of creativity in science that you have observed.

Read:

- Feasey, R (2003) 'Creative futures', *Primary Science Review*, 78, 21–23.
- Howe, A (2004) 'Science is creative', *Primary Science Review*, 81, 14–16.

Extract : Rutledge, N (2004) 'Genesis of the ice trolls', *Primary Science Review* **81, Jan/ Feb 2004. Hatfield: The Association for Science Education.**

Where creativity can enhance learning

The projects have shown that imagination and creativity can enhance learning in many ways but that the major area where it can have an impact is in the provision of a suitable learning context. Here five aspects should be considered:

1. Is the context fun? Will it motivate and enthuse the learners?
2. Is the context accessible? Will it make sense to the learners?
3. Is the context relevant? Does it provide learners with a reason to carry out their work?
4. Is the context appropriate? Does it support the necessary progression of skills and concepts?
5. Is the context flexible? Will it support differentiation and a cross-curricular approach?

If thought and imagination are put into these aspects, everything that follows is easier. These were the areas that were stressed during a partnership project to develop effective ways to help Year 4 children learn about thermal insulation.

A fun learning context

So were the Ice Trolls born! Small creatures bearing a passing resemblance to water-filled pop bottles with polystyrene spheres stuck on top, they inhabit the Icelandic glaciers, where, frozen solid, they live happy and innocuous lives. Faced with warmer temperatures, the Ice Trolls lose their cheery dispositions, sicken and melt.

Ice Trolls had a serious problem: global warming was making the glaciers recede and so they were losing their homes. They wanted to be able to travel and make a case to the governments of the world to address climate change but they were worried. They feared that once they left their special travelling compartments to meet people, they would quickly become ill and melt. The Trolls had heard the suggestion that if they clothed themselves, they would not melt so fast. They sought the children's help in finding out if this was the case.

Contact opened with the children having to politely invite, in Icelandic, the Ice Trolls out of their travelling compartment and then win their trust. This process made a very positive means of meeting each other, getting to know names and establishing behavioural expectations, etc. The children were instantly hooked and suspended their disbelief in the enchanting way that only children can.

An accessible and relevant learning context

The children clearly found the Ice Trolls to be fun but in addition they also made an accessible learning context. The anthropomorphic approach provided a context for the problem that the children could relate to more easily. They now had something concrete to think about when approaching the concepts involved and were more easily able to bring their own experience to bear on the problem. For the children it was like trying to help a friend. This also gave the context relevance. It was no alien hoop for the children to jump through, but an absorbing task that they treated with considerable urgency. The children themselves framed the project as 'Saving the Ice Trolls'.

An appropriate learning context

Science topics should certainly be fun and absorbing but they must also allow effective progression in developing concepts and this was certainly the case with the Ice Trolls. The manner in which the problem was framed immediately facilitated two of the most important components of science education. First there was an inbuilt opportunity to elicit the children's ideas. The Trolls themselves asked for the children's ideas – would clothing help or not? This allowed ample discussion, enabling the assessment of the children's understanding which, in turn, provided valuable information to aid the planning of further learning activities. The second linchpin of good practice is to allow the children to test their own ideas in an investigative manner. This was easy to facilitate, with the children designing investigations using the model proposed by Feasey and Goldsworthy (1997). The first investigation established that clothing the Trolls did indeed help them to stay frozen longer. Further investigation then explored what form of clothing was most effective. All of this not only allowed the children to progress their science skills, but also their understanding of thermal insulation.

Imaginative planning in response to the assessments of the children's ideas also demonstrated that the context could be taken further. Predictably some children were initially confused by the fact that they, unlike the Ice Trolls generated their own body heat. This led to the typical misconception that clothing actually produces heat and therefore the notion that clothing the Trolls would melt them more quickly. To help the children modify their views two extra learning activities were planned. The first involved some 'traditional' Icelandic folk dancing. This energetic activity allowed the children to quickly appreciate that their metabolism generated heat. In addition, it also provided an effective 'fill-in' activity as we waited to measure the results of our investigations. The other related activity involved the help of the Troll Twins, two identical large plastic Trolls, one wearing a fleece, and one without. This allowed the children to measure the twins' temperatures and to discover that it was the same, irrespective of cladding.

Analysis

The NACCCE (1999) defines teaching as *using imaginative approaches to make learning more interesting*. The underlying assumption here is that creative teaching will lead to creative learning. The delightful scenario above certainly meets this brief and is consistent with the development towards a more cross-curricular approach to learning.

Although motivation is the stated key reason for this approach, the Ice Trolls, without making this explicit, cleverly allow for the incorporation of environmental issues to be aired, thus tapping into the issue of global warming that we know is of interest to older children. While reading the article, a number of questions were raised that are worth considering. First, it is appropriate to ask whether enjoyment of science will necessarily lead to better science, or, for that matter, will a cross-curricular approach? The major justification for a 'fun' approach to science is linked to children's attitudes towards science. Further, how do we know that by taking this approach we are encouraging creativity in science? What are the characteristics of creative teaching that will lead to creative thinking in science? While there may be good motivational reasons for teaching creatively, does this necessarily achieve the objective of making children think creatively? Although motivation is said to be the key to creativity, motivation can come from a variety of origins. The extract provides a convincing argument for this approach but is this sort of approach realistically possible or even desirable? A creative approach to teaching should not be adopted just for the sake of it – there needs to be a purpose. Enjoyment and the 'fun' aspect of science has been advocated for many years for developing children's motivation, and no one would deny the role motivation plays in developing positive attitudes towards a subject.

There are important reasons why we should teach creatively, but these must not be at the expense of providing opportunities for creative thought. One criticism of the approach in the extract is that teaching should not seek to provide entertainment for children, while at the same time it is important that teachers adopt a variety of teaching approaches. However, not all of us are capable of being creative all the time in our planning and it would be very demanding and unrealistic for teachers to plan in this way all the time. Maybe there is no need, for in terms of teaching and in learning NACCCE (1999, p30) requires teachers to adopt a range of pedagogical skills. Children need to be interested and motivated to get optimum learning.

Does teaching creatively really go hand in hand with creative thinking? Should the emphasis be on providing opportunities for creative thinking? The move towards teaching for creativity encourages activities designed to make children independent and creative learners in order to develop their own creative thinking or behaviour. It is important to recognise that creating something is not the same as being creative. Being creative is how children are engaged, as well as the final product. This links back very nicely to the nature of science and the way science develops through practical activity and thought activities connected with these. Promoting children's creativity improves their self-esteem, motivation and achievement, develops individual talents and provides life skills.

Personal response

- Look back at your notes made from page 24 about creativity. How does your initial response concur with the views expressed in the extract?

- Think about your own practice after considering the extract. Do you take a creative approach to teaching science? If so, what are the characteristics of this aspect of your teaching?

- What do you think is the effect of your teaching style on your children's learning? Record some of the ways in which you have obtained a creative response from children in science.

Practical implications and activities

Task 1

Talk to your mentor. Share aspects of each of your practices and find examples of when you are teaching creatively. Does this happen in the teaching of science? If so, where?

Task 2

Teaching creatively is defined as *using imaginative approaches to make learning more interesting* (NACCCE 1999, p31-33) – teaching for creativity is concerned with planning activities that are designed to make children independent and creative learners.

Consider the above quotation. What sort of activities do you consider would achieve this objective?

Task 3

The move towards subject-based teaching has been criticised for limiting creativity, but would a move to a more cross-curricular approach necessarily lead to more creativity?

Task 4

Feasey's research (2003) found that many teachers link creativity with art, not science. Few teachers thought themselves as being creative in science teaching because the pressures of paperwork and assessment were stifling creativity. Teachers did not think that originality was a characteristic of creativity or that perseverance was associated with the characteristic of a creative child.

What is your reaction to these findings?

What arguments would you use to persuade such teachers to change their views?

Further reading

Harlen, W and Qualter, A (2004) 'Creative learning and creative teaching', in *The teaching of science in primary schools*. London: David Fulton.

Frost, J (1997) *Creativity in primary science*. Buckingham: Open University Press. This book provides case studies of teachers teaching creatively and shows the steps teachers make in planning for creative teaching. It also looks at how children's responses to the activities provided, e.g. in their recording, can be presented in a creative way.

How?

How can we recognise creativity in the learner?

Before you read the following extract, read:

- Harlen, W (2000) 'Children's learning', chapter 3, in *Teaching learning and assessing science 5-12*, 3rd ed. London: PCP.

Extract: Ovens, P (2004) 'A "SANE" way to encourage creativity'. *Primary Science Review* **81 Jan/Feb 2004, p17. Hatfield: The Association for Science Education.**

We notice children's creativity in their lively talk, practical ingenuity, funny or surprising ideas, or their new or clever ways of applying their knowledge. When the connections they make between ideas seem to come from them as individuals, there is a sense of authenticity. Understanding learning from a constructivist perspective emphasises the creativity of learning. Learners build new experiences into personal knowledge by deconstructing relevant bits of existing actions and understanding while constructing links with fresh ideas and new ways of doing things. Ultimately, only learners themselves can do this by their own efforts. Starting points for this process are practical experiences which arouse curiosity and raise questions … Can creativity and authenticity be recognised in the thinking that appears to be behind these questions?

The best person to judge the *authenticity* of these questions is the children's teacher, it seems clear that as authors of these questions the children have created possible links between what they already know and what they would like to learn next. In responding holistically, they have drawn upon their experiential knowledge and their emotional awareness, as well as their formal conceptual knowledge, to express their curiosity.

Treating children's questions with the care they deserve, as *emergent* objectives, is considered later. For now, it is worth emphasising that children's questions give a much better basis for constructivist teaching than *eliciting* children's concepts. Beginning a topic by asking children mainly closed questions about their conceptual knowledge in a context which is neither practical nor enquiring in character is not the ideal constructivist approach. This method tends only to elicit a part of *where the children are:* the science context which they *hold* it is unlikely to draw out their interests, curiosity, experiential knowledge and emotional aspects of their awareness. It may prevent learners from having some control over their own learning, which is fundamental both to constructivism and to creativity. It prioritises conceptual knowledge over experiential and personal kinds of knowledge. Worst of all, children's authentic curiosity and independent creative thinking may be killed 'stone-dead' if the teacher sets up the expectation that they control all the right answers on which the children's learning must converge.

Paul Waring-Thomas's (2001) action research (see also Ovens, 2000) was about *negotiating* with children on how to turn their authentic questions into plans for their own scientific enquiry. Through small–group discussion and using a planning frame, Paul challenged and extended their ideas. Control over the content of the lessons shuttled back and forth between the children and between them and Paul.

Encouraging children to be creative in science
Creativity is obviously more likely in situations which are open to a range of outcomes. If a single, fixed outcome is expected, a child's creative response may simply be excluded. Children who are not always determined to please the teacher, but who like to please themselves (in a positive sense of persevering with their own interests and meeting their own tacit 'standards' of achievement) may show creative responses

which seem to challenge the teacher's plan. Low achievers in numeracy and/or literacy may also be surprisingly creative … so the first point to make about teaching for creativity is that it must have sufficient openness to give *authentic opportunities* for children to be curious and to think independently. We must be open to what may *emerge* in children's responses to each situation. No teacher can predict with precision what *these* children who take *this* opportunity will say or do *now*. The appearance of creativity cannot be controlled. It cannot be elicited on demand like the recall of a correct answer to a closed question. Nor can it be predicted accurately across situations. So lessons cannot be planned in very great detail beforehand like set practical tasks. We cannot teach creativity by transmitting it or telling learners how to be creative.

Our role is to *stimulate* (encourage and challenge enquiry thinking), and elicit *authentic curiosity*. We temporarily relinquish some control over content while focusing on the children's constructive learning processes. Then our task is *negotiation* through discussion: of ideas, of purposes, of methods and meanings. In planning teaching for creativity, detailed and specific objectives must be *emergent*, not pre-specified. This is a SANE approach.

Analysis

Drawing evidence from children's own questions, Ovens (2004, p17) asks if creativity and authenticity can be recognised in the thinking that appears behind questions, and demonstrates how creativity in science can provide both 'excellence and enjoyment' while not being 'creative' in the way Rutledge suggests. The extract offers an attractive alternative view of 'creative teaching'. Ovens justifies this in terms of children's learning related not to fun and enjoyment, but to other aspects of creativity, such as independence and taking responsibility for their own learning. In doing so he draws out the essential elements of the science as a creative activity in its own right and harnesses this to develop children's ability to think creatively.

Ovens demonstrates clearly how children's curiosity and wanting to find out by investigating their own real, but negotiated questions is fostered very effectively within the teaching activity. Children are given time to think and respond without resorting to an imaginary scenario to promote interest and motivation. Here children's attitudes towards science would be fostered not through the 'fun' element (although the children were interested, stimulated and motivated), but through involvement in a real live context – in this case looking at living things and their needs.

Craft (2003) highlights the distinction between creative teaching and teaching for creativity. She offers the view that each of these are distinct from creative learning and that there is often a *slippage of the language in practice*, so that we may refer to creative teaching as teaching for creativity when it is not necessarily having this effect. Teaching creatively is not the same as developing the creative scientist, but how can we do this? What are the essential elements concerned with the development of the creative scientist?

It is possible to see aspects of science learning as being creative. For example, scientific investigation begins with observation or raising questions and science education seeks to foster this. Such learning can arise from curiosity and play in the learners' environment. Creative individuals continually question their actions and findings through this creative process. This is the method that Ovens adopts. In advocating this approach he is asking teachers to take risks, and, as we know, risk-taking is a fundamental aspect of creativity. This has to be true for both teachers and learners. In this context, *risk* does not mean putting in harm's way, but being prepared to follow a previously unexpected route. In the case of teachers, this means being prepared not always to know exactly what the outcome will be in any given situation. Teachers often fear this way of teaching. Many years ago one of my students compared this to entering a dark room and not liking what you might find there. Nevertheless, there are parallels here with meaningful learning in the Early Years classroom, particularly in relation to child-initiated play. Usually, the teacher's role in child-initiated play is to step back and observe, noting the outcomes of the experiences the child chooses to be involved in. Sometimes, the teachers involve themselves in the play. In some respects this can be likened to Ovens' negotiation of the questions for investigation in the extract.

For the very young child, learning begins with exploration, observation and play. This forms the basis for conceptual understanding, so that every child begins school with a basic understanding of science developed through their play and other activities particularly those that provide 'thinking time'. The Green Paper *Every Child Matters* (DfES 2003) places emphasis on enjoying and achieving. Theoretically, more freedom to explore, play and create will allow more time for the formation of both scientific and non-scientific ideas and, importantly, scope for the absorption of experience. Another point made in the extract is the need for consolidation and development of ideas, where children need space to think between times when they are active and manipulating materials.

The extract provides a very good example of a child making, what the teacher would consider to be the 'right' connection. However, creative ideas are sometimes (often) not considered to be the link the teacher wanted the child to make and creative ideas are at best dismissed and at worst discouraged. Take for example, Harlen's children working in the water tray. Here the children are exploring floating and sinking, but suddenly, in their explorations, discover that some of the blocks of wood stick together. They suggest that they are magnetic! Here the children are making links with previous ideas in a creative way. Although it would be easy to dismiss their ideas as being wrong, the two processes have similarities. It is very easy, as a teacher, to dampen signs of creativity by dismissing ideas, by not giving children the opportunity or time to think or to explain their train of thought.

Many teachers discourage creativity by viewing an unusual answer as disruptive or as a challenge to their authority, particularly when the teacher has insecure subject knowledge. Children who ask creative or unusual questions are sometimes labelled as difficult as a result. On the other hand a child who is doodling or playing with a pencil or not sitting on a chair properly coud be just thinking. It is easy to underestimate the quiet child. Often they do not have a chance to talk or are not asked to contribute, or are asked to contribute before ideas are fully formed. The teacher has to walk along a knife-edge between waiting for responses and insisting on a contribution.

You need to know your class well to know if a child is thinking and appearing not to be paying attention or, on the other hand, taking part in mental truancy.

In summary, the emphasis of teaching for creativity means schools should provide a stimulating environment where creativity will be promoted. Teachers need to expect the unexpected and develop work from the unexpected. The tasks below will provide you with an opportunity to reflect on the extent to which you meet this challenge.

Personal response

Have you asked the children to undertake a particular practical activity only to find that they have gone off at a tangent? If so, what was your reaction? What was the outcome?

Practical implications and activities

Task 1
Ask children to undertake a practical activity then stand back and watch them working with the materials provided.

Task 2

Visit QCA (2003) Creativity: find it, promote it (**www.ncaction.org.uk/ creativity**/) – accessed 2 June 2005

This website contains materials and resources designed to help teachers promote creativity. The materials were derived from existing schemes of work adapted to develop children's creativity. Interestingly, on the date accessed there were no examples matching a search for 'creativity and science'.

Look at the examples of work provided on the website. What view of science and science teaching do the examples suggest?

Share these with a colleague, then suggest the kinds of examples that would illustrate creativity in primary science.

Collect examples from your own teaching and share these with colleagues.

Further reading

Craft, A (2003) 'The limits to creativity in education: dilemmas for the educator'. *British Journal of Educational Studies*, 51 (2) 113-127.

3 The role of practical work

By the end of this chapter you should have:

- considered **why** practical work should be included in the primary science curriculum;
- reflected upon **what** role practical work plays in the learning of science;
- analysed **how** the discussion about the role of practical work can inform teaching in the primary classroom.

Linking your learning

Sharp, J, Peacock, G, Johnsey, R, Simon, S, and Smith, R *Achieving QTS: Primary science: teaching theory and practice.* Chapter 3. Exeter: Learning Matters.

Professional Standards for QTS
1.7, 2.1b, 3.3.2

Introduction

This chapter will explore the nature of scientific enquiry and how this is translated into practice within the National Curriculum. Scientific Enquiry (Sc1) is an important aspect of teaching and learning at Key Stages 1 and 2. While there has always been a requirement for teachers to assess children, until recently there has been the perception by teachers that the National Tests in Science have only assessed knowledge and understanding. Since 2003 there has been an increase in the number of test questions related to various aspects of scientific enquiry, for example, in which children are asked to plan an investigation or interpret given data from a practical activity.

There has been a long-standing and well-documented reluctance amongst some primary teachers to undertake practical activity with children. Many would argue that learning in science can be effectively achieved using text books and other secondary sources, indeed, you may be one of those successful teachers whose own experience of science has been 'book-based'. On the other hand there are many reports of children at primary level loving science. Much time and effort has been spent by teacher educators and enthusiastic science co-ordinators, first on trying to understand the reluctance of others to teach practical science, second on demonstrating and modelling how science can be taught, and third on providing well-planned and well-organised model lesson plans and resources.

While there may be many non-specialist teachers who question the reasoning behind the inclusion of practical work, few specialists stop to ask the fundamental question 'Why should we do practical work?' or ask, 'Is science really a practical subject?' Certainly some areas of science are very difficult to explore practically and evidence from other countries suggests that practical work may not warrant the emphasis given to it in British schools.

This chapter therefore takes this as its starting point and looks at the evidence to support the high profile and status given to science in the National Curriculum. Before this is explored it is important to make clear what is meant by practical work. There is a general consensus that practical work includes teaching or learning where children are involved in observation or manipulation of real objects in their environment. At the Foundation Stage, this would include exploration of the environment during free and structured play. Earlier chapters have made the point that science is more than just acquisition of knowledge, and that scientific enquiry is fundamental to the study of science. However, we need to be very clear about why we undertake practical work.

Why?

Why should practical work be included in the primary science curriculum?

Before you read the following extract, record your answers to these questions:

- what is your attitude towards practical activity?
- do you think practical activity is important to children's learning in science and, if so, why?

and read:

- Harlen, W (1998) 'A view of how children learn science', in *The teaching of science in primary schools,* 2nd edn. London: David Fulton.
- Harlen, W (1999) 'The role of practical work', chapter 2, in *Effective teaching of science: A review of research*, Edinburgh: SCRE.

Extract: Wellington, J (1998) 'Reasons for doing practical work now – and their limitations', in *Practical work in school science: which way now?* London: Routledge.

I recently asked a sample of 48 science graduates embarking on a teaching career to write down, on a small piece of paper, why we do practical work in school science. Inevitably I received a wide range of answers to such an open question, for example: 'to back up the theory'; 'to give pupils something to remember the theory by'; 'to make theory more visual and accessible to kids'; 'makes things easier to remember'; 'to give experience – seeing is believing'; 'to bring science to life'; 'develop manipulative skills'; 'to develop skills useful to life and to home'; 'to develop practical skills'; 'to develop an enquiring mind'; 'to learn transferable skills like a fair test, or planning and observation'. On a more practical level some wrote 'to make a change from theory work'; 'something else to do apart from lessons'; 'keep kids quiet'; 'make lessons more interesting'; 'they break up lessons to keep the kids entertained'; 'fun – sometimes!'; 'nice change'; 'to make boring, dry topics more fun'; 'give interest and variety'.

This wide range of responses is interesting to consider in the light of research … My own reading of the literature is that the reasons and rationales put forward can be grouped into three main areas: one relating to knowledge and understanding (the cognitive domain); one relating to skills and processes, often deemed to be transferable; and the third relating to attitudes enjoyment and motivation (the affective domain). I found it interesting that all the free range responses given by learner teacher fall into these three groups.

1. *Cognitive arguments:* it is argued that practical work can improve pupils' understanding of science and promote their conceptual development by allowing them to 'visualise' the laws and theories of science. It can illustrate, verify or affirm 'theory' work.

The counter argument to this, of course, is that practical work can confuse as easily as it can clarify or aid understanding (especially if 'it goes wrong') hence the counter slogan … 'I do and I become confused'. It can be argued that theory comes first and is needed in order to visualise – not the other way round: experience does not give concepts meaning, if anything, concepts give experience meaning (Theobald, 1968).

This may be a good argument for doing practical work after teaching and discussing theory but practical work is still not a good tool for teaching theory – theories are about ideas, not things. Theories involve abstract ideas which cannot be physically illustrated: 'in the context of the school laboratory it is clear that students cannot develop an understanding through their own observations, as the theoretical entities of science are not there to be seen' (Leach and Scott, 1995, p48).

2. *Affective arguments:* practical work, it has been argued, is motivating and exciting – it generates interest and enthusiasm. It helps learners to remember things, it helps to 'make it stick'.

Few who have taught science would deny this. But this is not the case for all pupils – some are 'turned off' by it, especially when it goes wrong or they cannot see the point of doing it. All teachers can relate to the lovely quote from the pupil in Qualter *et al.* (1990, p5), 'Oh no, Sir! Not another one of your problems', as she responds to her teacher's attempt to turn a piece of practical work into a 'problem-solving' investigation. Evidence from Murphy in Woolnough (1991) indicates that more girls than boys react negatively to practical work in science.

3. *Skills arguments:* it is argued that practical work develops not only manipulative or manual dexterity skills, but also promotes higher-level, transferable skills such as observation, measurement, prediction and inference. These transferable skills are said not only to be valuable to future scientists, but also to possess general utility and vocational value.

There may be some truth in the claim for manipulative skills and possibly measurement, but there is little evidence that skills learned in science are indeed general and transferable or that they are of vocational value.

In a slightly different area of skill (personal skills and teamwork) it has been claimed that the small group work which inevitably goes on in practical science can develop such skills as communication, interaction and co-operation. Again, this may be partially true, but when group work is closely observed and analysed it often reveals domination by forceful members, competition, lack of engagement for some, and a division of tasks which may leave one pupil simply recording results or drawing out a neat table without even seeing, let alone touching, any apparatus.

Analysis

This extract and that of Harlen (1999) drew largely from research into secondary education. Contrary to the beliefs of enthusiasts, there are certainly similarities between what critics say about practical work and the issues raised in the extract. Taking an objective stance, some aspects of the extract 'ring true' and deserve further reflection. So, it is pertinent to ask why practical work should be included in the primary science curriculum.

Wellington considers the relationship between practical work and understanding. It is often assumed that 'practical work' is worthwhile in its own right without considering the nature of the practical. The term 'practical work' relates to a whole range of activities in primary science, from those that provide the opportunity to practise and develop skills (e.g. observation and question-raising) to illustrative work and planning and carrying out whole investigations. Although it would never be the intended outcome, there is always the possibility that practical work will reinforce rather than challenge misconceptions. It is pertinent to ask why and how this might happen. Could it be, for example, that the teacher has not allowed time to find out what exactly the children have learned from the practical activity? If so, what needs to be done about this?

Wellington also states that theories cannot be physically illustrated. If this is correct, what are we really aiming for when children carry out practical work? What is the 'real' purpose? Almost every teacher must have experienced the 'experiment' that didn't work. How can this be avoided? Is it always a disaster if an experiment 'doesn't work'? What do we mean by 'experiment' anyway?

The extract raises even more questions. Do pupils really become 'turned off' science? If so, why does this happen? Do girls and boys approach practical activities in different ways? What evidence supports the view that as girls become older, they are put off science because of the practical work? Is this observation common? In relation to the skills argument, is there evidence to support the view that the skills involved in science do not have vocational value? Is group work really dominated by forceful members, competition, lack of engagement for some, etc.? If so, why is this case? What is the role of the teacher here? What can be done to make practical work more effective? Finally, if we were not to place so much emphasis on practical work in the Foundation Stage and Key Stages 1 and 2 what would be put in its place? Alternatively, if practical work cannot be justified, would science be better delivered in some other form? If so, what would this look like?

Personal response

Are you one of those teachers who would like to see the end of practical work in the primary school or do you take issue with the points raised?

- How do your thoughts and feelings on the matter concur with that presented in the extract?
- What other questions might you raise in relation to the extract?

Note down your responses.

Practical implications and activities

Task 1

Fundamental to the National Curriculum is the notion that science is a practical subject. However, we know that practical work can be time-consuming in an already overcrowded primary curriculum.

Talk to a science co-ordinator about this issue, then:

- With a colleague, discuss and make a note of all the reasons for the inclusion of practical work in science at the Foundation Stage, and at Key Stages 1 and 2.
- What is it about practical work that is so attractive to many in primary education?
- Write down three key things that could help to make practical work more effective.
- What steps do you think must be taken to ensure that practical science succeeds in what it sets out to do?

Task 2

Much practical work is beneficial, but some wastes time and confuses children. Practical work *can* be routine, dull, demotivating and boring.

- Can you think of an occasion when you or one of the children has become more confused by undertaking practical work? If so, can you identify the source of the problem?
- Referring your notes made while reading the extract, observe a group of children undertaking practical work. Is there any evidence to support the views above in your classroom?
- Talk to other trainees about this issue. What are your findings?

Task 3

You may be one of those trainees, or know others who are involved in the Primary Modern Foreign Language initiative. In your/their experience, how does the role of practical work vary from country to country?

Further reading

Solomon, J, (1998) 'Science education from a European perspective', chapter 1.5, in Sherrington, R *ASE guide to primary science education.* Hatfield: ASE Cheltenham: StanleyThornes.

Britain has a history of including practical work in school science, but other countries tend not to. Solomon explores the similarities and differences in science education across Europe and considers the reasons why, in 1998, the British system of education was the only one in Europe to have compulsory assessed practical work and required pupils to perform investigations.

What?

What role does practical work play in learning science?

Before you read the following extract, read:

- Harlen, W (1998) 'The last ten years; the next ten years', chapter 1.3, in Sherrington, R (1998) *ASE guide to primary science education.* Hatfield: ASE Cheltenham: StanleyThornes.

Extract: Armstrong, H E (1902) 'Training in scientific method as a central motive in elementary schools', in Van Praagh, G (ed.) (1973) *H E Armstrong and science education*. London: John Murray.

The proposition I desire to submit today is that the central ideas – the central motive – in elementary schools should be to give training in scientific method. Some, perhaps many, will be inclined to hold up their hands in horror. To teach science at all, they say, is unnecessary: to urge that it should be the central subject is preposterous … I am not here to advocate the introduction into the school of *science* in the ordinary acceptation of the term. For years, in fact, I have objected to the teaching of specific branches of science and have contended for something more general – that training should be given which tends to develop what are becoming to be known as scientific habits of mind, i.e. thoughtfulness and power of seeing, accuracy of thought, of word and of deed.

It is unfortunate that the words science and scientific are but disguised Latin words which scarcely convey any clear meaning to most people as they refer to something unfamiliar … it is perhaps easier to understand them if we translate the words into German and then back into Anglo-Saxon. The German equivalent of our word science is 'Wissenschaft' – the business of knowing. To be scientific is to be knowing or canny, in the best and highest and fullest sense of the term: the knowing man being one who *can* – who has the power of doing, producing as well as holding. Surely, no one can object to becoming scientific, if such be the meaning of the term: all will wish to be scientifically inclined.

Absence of imaginative power seems to be at the root of our difficulties; and consequently we are both apathetic and prejudiced. Perhaps nothing is more important at the present time than that teachers should cultivate the power of imagination. To get back upon the rails, we must treat the problem scientifically – with true knowingness.

We must consider most carefully what is the material to be dealt with and what we are to aim at; and then see how our object can be gained. The material to be dealt with is an active young animal whose healthy natural desire is to rove about and be inquisitive about things generally; to dissect and to get at the inside of things; a young animal full of latent ability and with strongly marked practical tendencies. Instead of developing his natural instincts, his imaginative power and his individuality, we glue him to a desk and cram him with mere facts – mainly from books. We practically shut him off from the world outside and we scarcely allow him to handle anything: the instinct to experiment, which is so highly developed in children, is almost if not altogether disregarded. There is neither common sense nor morality in such a system!

The teacher of the future must be guide, philosopher and friend to the taught – not a mere trainer of parrots … he must cut himself adrift from codes, and become a self-acting, reasoning being, prepared to see and use his opportunities – not a mere automaton wound up once for all at a training college.

We are so accustomed to our eyes, that we fail to recognise that eyes must be taught if they are to see properly … that they are to see with a greater intelligence than a photographic plate; that they need to be trained to interpret not only written or printed signs but also the signs in the great book of Nature around us.

And although we value experience, we scarcely recognise that the habit of asking questions and some skill in obtaining answers to such questions by mean of experiments – the art of gaining experience, in fact – is one which needs the most careful cultivation if it is to be carried to any degree of perfection … But the great object of the teacher of science should be to teach the *art of experimenting* – the meaning and use of an experiment. Therefore, the motive with which each experiment is made must be clearly understood; the best way of making it must be thought out; it must be made deliberately; the result must be carefully noted. Finally, the bearing of the result - the extent to which it affords an answer to the question asked – must be considered; if the answer be not satisfactory or complete, other experiments must be devised … In teaching children to experiment, a teacher must exercise extraordinary self-restraint in withholding information; however slowly the argument may develop, it *must be allowed* to develop solely on the basis of the facts established in the course of the inquiry … teachers are not trained at present to work in such a spirit – but more's the pity, more's the shame! To make our teaching something else than parrot training, the teacher must be imbued with the spirit of the discoverer. A teacher who tries to force himself to work from such a point of view may experience great difficulty at first – but if he but persevere, he will sooner or later succeed and what will astonish him most will be the growth in his own power.

Analysis

Armstrong is often said to be the 'father of popular science education'. As this short extract demonstrates, he held very strong ideas about education in general, teacher education and science education in particular. At first glance you might be forgiven for thinking that Armstrong was contributing to the current discussions about the future direction of science education in the twenty-first century. However, this particular extract was written in 1902 in a context very different from our own, so it is pertinent to ask 'What relevance do his writings have today?'

We need to step back to explore and try to understand the context in which he was writing. What was Britain like at the beginning of the twentieth century and what was popular education like? What are the similarities and differences? At that time Britain was prosperous, reaping the benefits of the industrial revolution. Popular education was introduced under the 1870 Education Act in response to legislation that had taken children out of the world of work and onto the streets. Why should his views be relevant to today? What are the characteristics of modern society? What are the needs of modern society? What sort of science education should we be aiming for? What are the messages that we can consider in relation to our own social context, and the education system which underpins it? Armstrong's ideas seem to echo in debates raging today.

On the role of the teacher, Armstrong held radical views for his day. What message does Armstrong provide about the role of the teacher in teaching science? Can teachers really be accused of being 'mere trainers of parrots'? Can this be recognised in any part of science education today? Is there any evidence that this approach is adopted in the primary schools of today? Also, the 'process verses content' debate seems to have been of interest then. Why had this not been settled years ago? Why should this have been focused on scientific 'method' that we would call scientific enquiry? Then, as today he was advocating practical work although it might be time consuming and possible atypical of practice then.

His exploration of what the word science means, and therefore what a study of science should entail could be significant today along with his views about 'the absence of imaginative power'. What messages is he giving to the wider education community? Armstrong talks of children exploring the world around them, looking with 'seeing' eyes, asking questions, interpreting data. What is the role of these aspects that we would call process skills? Although he does not use modern terms, you can see elements currently being debated.

Personal response

Compare and contrast Armstrong's view of scientific method with that of your own.

What parallels do you see between Armstrong's portrayal of the child as 'an active young animal' and your own beliefs about the nature of the child?

Practical implications and activities

Make a note of the key points from the above extract.

Compare these with your responses.

- In the light of analysis of this and the previous extract, what role does practical work play in primary science?

Further reading

Armstrong, H E (1902) 'Training in scientific method as a central motive in elementary schools', in Van Praagh, G (1973) (ed) *H E Armstrong and science education,* London: John Murray.

It is really worthwhile reading the whole article for, as Van Praagh (writing in 1973) said, *Armstrong's views are so relevant to aspects of science teaching that are being actively being discussed today.* In fact, his ideas went far beyond that relating to science education because he was also advocating, with examples, highly detailed ideas for cross-curricular work. Clearly, these issues are not only of interest today but are relevant to the discussions that will contribute to the 'Teaching Futures' debate as we move towards 2020.

How?

How does the discussion about the role of practical work inform practice?

Before you read the following extract, read:

- Harlen, W and Qualter, A (2004) 'Experiences that promote learning in science', chapter 5, in *The teaching of science in primary schools,* London: David Fulton.

Extract: Wenham, M (2005) 'The relevance of scientific investigation', *Understanding primary science, ideas, concepts and explanations,* **2nd edition, pp 3–4. London: Sage Publications.**

The relevance of scientific investigation

In the primary school scientific knowledge and understanding are not only, nor even principally, about other people's discoveries. An important and integral part of primary education is to help children develop the ability to investigate things for themselves: to perceive problems, think up possible answers, find out whether their ideas stand up to testing and communicate their findings clearly. Scientific investigation has an important and direct contribution to make to this process, but it also has a wider relevance in helping to develop a critical awareness of science and its influence within the community.

As far as anyone can predict, the lives of children who are in primary schools today will be affected even more by science than the lives of their teachers and parents are at present. There is an obvious need for as many people as possible not only to understand something of the scientific knowledge and theory which affects their lives, but also to be critical of scientists' claims. Critical evaluation of any kind of knowledge or discovery is impossible unless one knows how the results were arrived at. This is because, in any kind of investigation, results and ways of working depend on and shape each other. What is discovered depends not only on what is investigated, but also on the methods used … and the ideas knowledge and experience of the investigator. This means that first-hand investigations are relevant and valuable not only because they develop knowledge, understanding and the ability to investigate competently, but also because they help to give children a more realistic insight into how science works, its achievements and (equally important) its limitations.

Analysis

As we have seen, explaining the role of practical work is not as clear cut as it might seem. But it is important that we have a clear view of its nature and role to get the balance right. You need to understand how the different forms of practical work can be used effectively to support learning in science. Different kinds of practical work are appropriate for different purposes. Not only does practical work need to be hands on, minds on and possibly 'ears' on, but also we need to ensure that children are active learners and not just kept busy with tasks that keep their hands occupied.

In the extract, Wenham provides a clear justification for the inclusion of scientific investigation as part of the primary science curriculum, and brings us back to issues raised in Chapter 1 when the need for the development of a scientifically literate society was examined.

Personal response

Write down your current view of practical work after reading the above.

- Look back at your response to the first task at the beginning of the chapter. Have your views changed?

Practical implications and activities

Task 1
Take another look at chapter 3 of Sharp *et al.* (2002), *Primary science: teaching theory and practice.*

List the different forms of practical work included. Make a brief note of the role of each.

Task 2
Take a look at your current scheme of work or the one you most recently worked with.

- Highlight the parts of the scheme that involved practical work.
- Identify the nature of the practical work involved in each.
- Match each identified activity with its corresponding learning objective or intended outcome.
- Analyse the scheme for its use of practical work.
- What conclusions do you draw about the opportunities the scheme offers for children's learning in science?
- In the light of your current understanding of the role of practical work could changes be made to improve the purpose and clarity of the activities provided?

Further reading

Wenham, M (2005) 'Science: investigation, invention and experiment', chapter 1 in *Understanding primary science*, 2nd edn. London: Paul Chapman Publishing.

4   Scientific enquiry

By the end of this chapter you should have:

- considered **why** it is important to be clear about what sort of science education is appropriate for our children towards 2020;
- reflected upon **what** teaching for procedural understanding entails;
- analysed **how** teachers can provide opportunities for the development of procedural understanding in the primary classroom.

Linking your learning

Sharp, J, Peacock, G, Johnsey, R, Simon, S, and Smith, R (2002) *Achieving QTS. Primary science: teaching theory and practice.* Chapter 3. Exeter: Learning Matters.

Professional Standards for QTS
1.7, 2.1b, 3.3.1, 3.3.2

Introduction

You will be familiar with the role of process skills in science. These are the skills that very young children use naturally as they explore the world in a practical way. Science process skills have long been promoted within primary science education and are fundamental to Sc1 Scientific Enquiry within the National Curriculum 2000 (DfES, 1999). Understanding how children develop individual process skills can enable you to provide a firm basis for the development of their ability to engage with materials in a scientific way. Many of the skills are not exclusive to science, but are important for furthering children's knowledge and understanding of science.

Scientific enquiry has a number of aspects within the National Curriculum. There is an expectation that children will be taught to observe and ask questions, but there is also the requirement for children to engage in more demanding practical work where a range of process skills are used together. There is, however, often a tendency for teachers to provide activities in science rather than to choose activities to meet specific learning outcomes related to scientific enquiry. The science National Curriculum requires children to build up their understanding of science alongside their ability to work in a scientific manner. As Sharp *et al.* (2002) point out, *learning the way that scientists work can help pupils understand the basis for decisions in an increasingly technological world; that through science pupils can develop skills to help them solve problems and discover that science is interesting and intellectually stimulating.* The challenge for you is to develop the necessary understanding of how to promote this aspect of science in your classroom. Scientific development progresses from unstructured exploration prior to and during the Foundation Stage to more systematic practical investigation at the top end of Key Stage 1 and beyond. Within this process, children need to look for scientific explanations when interpreting collected data. An important point to note here is that children's scientific knowledge will develop, though not exclusively, through engaging in practical scientific enquiry.

This chapter sets out to enable you to reflect on the kind of science education that is really needed and will explore how teachers can engage children in the procedures of science. It will provide pointers for reflecting on action and present some of the problems associated with teaching this aspect of the National Curriculum Programme of Study.

Why?

Why is it important to be clear about what sort of science education is appropriate for our children as we move towards 2020?

Before you read the following extract, read:

- Harlen, W (2000) 'Children's learning experiences', chapter 6 in *Teaching learning and assessing science 5-12*, London: Paul Chapman Publishing.

Extract: Duggan, S and Gott, R (2002) 'What sort of science education do we really need?', *International Journal of Science Education,* **24 (7), pp661-679. London: Taylor & Francis Ltd.**

Introduction

That there are problems with the content of the science curriculum, at least in the UK, is widely recognised and epitomised by a recent survey of pupils' perceptions (Osborne and Collins, 2000) which highlighted, amongst other things, the fragmented and disjointed picture of science that many pupils receive. The pupils' responses, the authors write, suggest that:

> the school science curriculum is failing to construct a coherent picture of the subject, its methods and its practices, leaving pupils with fragmented pieces of knowledge (p30).

There is also the agreement that the science curriculum is overloaded. These, together with the perceptions of pupils that science is 'difficult' and that it lacks relevance to everyday life, are some of the factors thought to account for the demotivation of students towards science as they move through compulsory education and to contribute to the fact that most opt out of studying science at higher levels.

In addition there is ongoing concern about the scientific literacy of the general population arising from surveys of the public understanding of science. The relationship between the science curriculum and the preparation it provides in enabling pupils to apply their understanding of science to topical science-based issues is in question (see e.g. Fensham 1998). Bayliss (1999) challenges the traditional model of education ... She points to the need for greater creativity and imagination and the recent interest in aptitude tests rather than in exams which are seen to reward, to a large extent, rote recall. At the same time, the growth of consumerism and the move towards evidence-based policy and decision making in many aspects of life mean that there is a shift in the relationship between science and the public. As controversial science-related issues emerge and the uncertain nature of science is clearly exposed, the public are being confronted with science in ways that they were not in the past.

What sort of knowledge of science does the population really need?

Implications for science education

In relation to science-based employment, the results reported here confirm earlier research indicating that conceptual and procedural knowledge are both important in the workplace. Our findings provide more detail about each of these 'limbs' of science.

Procedural understanding

In the industries we studied there were a number of fundamental concepts such as an understanding of the choice of an appropriate instrument, repeatability, error and accuracy that most industries in the sample required. Understanding these ideas and the wider concepts of validity and reliability were highly valued.

1. Pupils need to know and understand the principle concepts of evidence and the overarching concepts of validity and reliability. A secure knowledge of procedural understanding appeared to be critical … The ability to sift through evidence, recognise when it was 'good' evidence or recognise where there was no evidence were crucial in action groups and in informed personal decision making. Understanding concepts such as risk and uncertainty were also crucial.
2. Pupils need to know how to use and apply concepts of evidence such that they can critically evaluate scientific evidence. It is noticeable that it was those who pursued science at higher levels who appeared to exhibit sound procedural understanding both in industry and everyday life, so they were in a position to handle evidence confidently and effectively … It seems that the more able pupils with an aptitude for science do indeed pick up procedural understanding in the course of their science education, but this is not the case for the majority. Previous research (Foulds *et al.*, 1992) has shown that the majority of pupils leave school with a poor understanding of evidence suggesting that repeated exposure to practical work is insufficient and that explicit teaching of procedural understanding is necessary.

Conceptual understanding

The results of our research indicate that, beyond basic concepts, most of the conceptual understanding required is specific to a particular industry such that it should not be feasible or sensible to incorporate all such knowledge into the curriculum. In any case, some particular bits of expertise are transitory while others are relatively new or developing rapidly. Employees gain company-specific knowledge in the workplace and some is probably best learned when seen 'in action', for example, in manufacturing or in developing a real product.

The results of our exploration of science in everyday life confirmed earlier research indicating that the public can access and acquire specific conceptual knowledge when motivated to do so in relation to a particular problem of immediate and direct concern. Our findings also show that the public makes good use of the internet which has made the accessibility of relevant specific and up-to-date conceptual knowledge immeasurably easier.

Much of science-based industry and science-based issues that concern the public concerns 'new science', so, for example, the concern is about new technology or new processes which impinge on society. Hence industry's desire to burn recycled liquid fuel or the erection of mobile phone base stations are issues which did not exist ten years ago when most of the adults involved in the action groups were receiving their science education. In this respect, science curricula cannot expect to keep up to date with all aspects of science, but can only aspire to teach pupils how to access and critically evaluate such knowledge. It follows that:

1. Pupils need to know how to: access conceptual knowledge which is directly relevant to topical issues; apply and use such knowledge in 'real' issues.

Recommendations for curricular reform
The results from both industry and science in everyday life suggest that there should be a greater emphasis on the explicit teaching of procedural understanding and on the teaching of conceptual content … far from not teaching the basics of science, we believe that procedural understanding lies at the heart of scientific literacy and is the sort of science education that adults really need.

Analysis

Your reaction to the extract might be to ask what relevance does this have to primary practice? Duggan and Gott's article aims primarily to inform a review of the science curriculum at Key Stages 3, 4 and beyond, but it is relevant to primary not least because the primary curriculum provides children with the foundation upon which to build their knowledge, skills and attitudes post Year 6. Furthermore, there is also a need to review the content and the teaching methods employed at primary level to ensure the optimum preparation for the study of science beyond the primary school.

Duggan and Gott raise a number of key issues to be explored at the primary level. The first relates to the content of science and the second to whether children are receiving a fragmented curriculum lacking in coherence. They also emphasise the need for procedural understanding to form a significant part of the science curriculum, but what exactly is meant by this term? Roden and Ward (2005, p3) tell us that procedural knowledge is one of the four strands of science alongside conceptual understanding, skills and attitudes that are linked and vital if science is to continue to have any relevance for children in the twenty-first century. Without this breadth, science can be a dry and limiting subject which fails to interest and excite and is reduced to a list of facts to be learned and experiments to be conducted. So, procedural knowledge is more than just skills and includes elements of the nature of science and the development of scientific ideas.

Scientific understanding proceeds, develops and changes by questioning the validity and reliability of scientific 'truths' often accepted as scientific 'facts'. Such questions result in the testing of hypotheses in order to validate or invalidate these and can often be tested by practical activity. It is appropriate then that primary children should engage in this aspect of science, to develop an understanding of the nature of science alongside the development of individual process skills and scientific understanding, which is part of the essential aspects of developing a scientifically literate individual.

What of the content of primary science? Is it overloaded? If so, what could be left out? We know that scientific knowledge changes as time goes by, so what was taught in the twentieth century may not now be relevant. Are primary children merely collecting a 'fragmented picture of science knowledge' or are they able to make the links for themselves? How could we find out? Perhaps children's performance on National Tests could give us answers to these questions. Do we help children make the necessary links? If not, how can this be done? Do our children become demotivated as they get older in primary schools? If so, why is this the case?

Duggan and Gott raise another pertinent point. Today it is possible for children to access information from the internet in a way not possible even ten years ago. So, is it more important for primary children to be able to answer questions to test their recall of scientific facts, or for them to be able to find information, weigh up evidence, come to a conclusion and decide what is relevant? In other words is it better to 'know that' or to 'know how'? What do you think?

Personal response

Duggan and Gott ask 'What sort of science education do we really need?' Reflect on this question and on the following:

- What do you consider to be the essential content of the primary science curriculum?
- What sorts of activities will promote positive attitudes towards science for both boys and girls and hence lead to a more scientifically literate population?

As a result of your own reflection on the extract, what further questions could you add to extend the debate?

Practical implications and activities

Compare and contrast the ideas raised in this extract with current practice in a school known to you. What aspects are included and what is excluded?

- What action needs to be taken to ensure that children in primary schools receive the right kind of science education?
- Explore the children's attitudes towards science. Try to find out what factors are influencing this situation.
- Consider the way in which a school, that you know well, attempts to develop scientific literacy.

Further reading

Barker, V (2000) 'Lifelong learning in science: dream or reality?', chapter 6, in Sears, J and Sorensen, P (2000) *Issues in science education.* London: RoutledgeFalmer.

Turner, T (2000) 'The science curriculum: what is it for?', chapter 1, in Sears, J and Sorensen, P (2000) *Issues in science education.* London: RoutledgeFalmer.

What?

What does teaching for procedural understanding entail?

Before you read the following extract, read:

- Ellis, S and Kleinberg, S (2000) 'Exploration and enquiry', chapter 3, in de Boo (ed) *Laying the foundations in the early years,* Hatfield: ASE.

Extract: Ward, H (2005) 'Scientific enquiry', chapter 5, in Ward, H, Roden, J, Hewlett, C and Foreman, J (2005) *Teaching science in the primary classroom: a practical guide*. London: Sage Publications Ltd.

The importance of scientific enquiry

The focus of science teaching has most recently centred upon the knowledge and understanding of science at the expense of investigative and illustrative processes because of the emphasis upon Year 6 pupils attaining Level 4 in National Tests. As a result many pupils receive a very bland and boring diet of science involving comprehension tasks. In recent years the lack of investigative approaches has been commented upon in a number of forums from parliamentary reports (2003), OFSTED publications (OFSTED/HMI, 2002; 2003; 2004) and the professional press. Time pressure, a testing arrangement that appeared to favour what was 'easy to test' rather than 'what is science', together with the introduction of 'the National Primary Strategies', have all contributed to the current position. It is possible, indeed, there is an opportunity, that the changes to the tests initiated in 2003 might help to refocus science teaching. Investigative work is, more than any activity, one that involves equipment and practical tasks. The following are the stages of scientific enquiry:

1. Selection of the global question.*
2. Identification of the independent variables.
3. Thinking of how to measure/observe the outcome (dependent variable).
4. Question generation.
5. Selecting the equipment and deciding how to use it.
6. Deciding what might happen (making a predication) if needed.*
7. Data collection methods – type and amount of data to be collected.*
8. Making observations and measurements.
9. Recording and evaluating the data (reliability).
10. Interpreting the data.
11. Drawing conclusions.
12. Evaluating the process.*

* *Using secondary sources of information can occur at a number of points. It will differ according to the investigation as well as age of pupils, but is an important part of the process.*

It can be seen that there are many steps, and when undertaking an investigation the pupils will follow and be involved in all the steps. In illustrative work steps 1–5 will be undertaken by the teacher. This is perhaps why pupils make so many predictions as this is the first part of the process where they can be involved. Basic skill lessons focus on only one step at a time, as discussed in detail in Chapter 2. The term 'investigation' is used explicitly for activities, which require pupils to think and make choices about 'what to vary' and 'what to measure'. It is this *choice* that is important as it enables the pupils to plan their own work. In investigative work pupils plan by selecting the variable (factor) they will change and then deciding how to measure and record the effect of the changes. The pupils then carry out the whole process of investigating their own idea, using basic skills they have acquired. Illustrative work is important as it enables pupils to learn about science in a practical way by focusing upon a limited number of skills at any one time. Such work enables pupils to change or vary factors and to measure or observe effects, but the 'what to do' and the 'how to do it' is prescribed by the teacher. Illustrative science allows pupils to arrive at the expected outcome as it is teacher directed at most stages. Due to the formal nature of the illustration it is easy to focus pupils' attention directly upon what is required. The methods of communication and recording are also prescribed in illustrative work, and the activities undertaken provide experiences upon which future investigations can be based. Illustrative work provides opportunities for pupils to experience aspects of scientific enquiry. It is a myth that pupils will become investigative scientists by a process similar to osmosis, picking up skills, attitudes and concepts by 'being there'! Pupils generate ideas and questions but enabling them to answer these questions in a scientific way requires procedural understanding to be developed throughout the primary age range. The process should be started in the early years and the degree of challenge and the complexity of tasks increased as pupils progress through the school. In order to be successful there needs to be a common approach across the school, with all adults working in similar ways. This is known as continuity, and without a continuous approach it is unlikely that pupils' learning will progress. In order to make this easier to manage there needs to be agreement about progression in procedural understanding which will result in all teachers knowing what pupils have already been taught and where they are expected to progress next. This is easier to achieve if the expectation for ways of working in all aspects of science are clearly stated for each year group. From a simple starting point in early years, pupils will develop more independence. The level descriptions (Attainment Target 1) make it clear where progress should be focused at each level through the key stages. Using this information together with extensive opportunities to work with pupils in whole-class investigative activities and in real settings allowed a suggested framework for progression to be constructed.

The list above provides an opportunity for teachers to gain an understanding of where the age range they teach fits within the whole schemata and is a starting point for future discussion in schools. The theory supporting this framework has as the central tenet that pupils will make gains in understanding and skills, if development is in small steps and there is support from teachers and others. For pupils to be successful, teachers have continually to aim to extend unaided achievement, by planning small steps and increasing the challenge. This is only effective when all teachers work to the same goals and realistic but challenging expectations are set from the start. It also requires a belief in the importance of procedural understanding.

Analysis

Ward is very clear in her view of worthwhile scientific enquiry in the primary class-room, but a number of statements in the extract need to be explored and, if necessary, challenged. For example, is it really true that many children receive a boring diet of science involving comprehension tasks? Has the National Primary Strategy had a detri-mental effect on the teaching of science? What has been the effect of the change to the National Tests in science from 2003?

Further, Ward tells us that investigative work is more than an activity that involves equipment and practical tasks. It is easy, however, for teachers to do just that and to feel that they are providing the right opportunities for their children, but is this the case? Do teachers engage the children in a whole range of activities that contribute to their procedural understanding? Ward provides a framework for the development of procedural understanding based on scientific enquiry, but clearly this is more than chil-dren undertaking fair test investigation. In the list, you will notice the inclusion of elements such as recording and evaluating the data which is a requirement of the National Curriculum. This is one of the higher-level skills and needs to be taught speci-fically. Implicit in this requirement of stages of scientific enquiry is that time needs to be allocated for children to collect and make sense of their own collected data. There is also a clear need to practise a whole range of associated skills such as asking their own questions, making observations and measurements, drawing conclusions and eval-uating the process.

The extract also emphasises children's need for choice. This is possible at almost every stage of the process, but how much choice do teachers usually provide? Is this an area of weakness that needs to be addressed? The roles of illustrative and investigative science are also explored in the extract. It is very easy to present an idea to children either as an illustrative task or an investigation. Teachers need to be aware of the differ-ent nature of each and understand the differing opportunities they provide. Do they address both these aspects of scientific enquiry in their schemes of work? Do they understand what is meant by procedural understanding and how they can develop learning in this area?

Personal response

What is your reaction to Ward's view of science in many schools? To what extent does your experience confirm or disprove this scenario?

Practical implications and activities

With a colleague review a scheme of work for science for a particular year group familiar to you.

- Identify where scientific enquiry is located. Is there any evidence of English masquerading as science?
- Is there evidence of the time and tasks to facilitate procedural knowledge as outlined in the extracts above? Is specific time allocated to children analysing data and drawing their own conclusions, or are children merely required to undertake practical work, as Ward describes?

Further reading

Feasey, R (1998) 'Scientific investigations in context', chapter 2.3, in Sherrington, R (Ed) *ASE guide to primary science education*. Hatfield: ASE/Stanley Thornes.

Warwick P, Sparks, R, Stephenson, P and Stephenson L (1999) 'A comparison of primary school pupils' ability to express procedural understanding in science through speech and writing', *International Journal of Science Education* 21 (8): 823-838.

How?

How can teachers provide opportunities for the development of procedural understanding?

Before you read the following extract, read:

- Goldsworthy, A (1998) 'Learning to investigate', chapter 2.2, in Sherrington, R (ed) *ASE guide to primary science education*. Hatfield: ASE/Stanley Thornes.

Extract: Watson, R, Goldsworthy, A and Wood-Robinson, V (2000) 'Sc1 beyond the fair test', chapter 8, Sears, J, and Sorensen, P *Issues in Science Education*. **London: RoutledgeFalmer.**

Introduction

How do scientists carry out scientific investigations? There is no straightforward answer to this question. Scientists use a great range of investigative approaches. For example, they carry out laboratory tests, study patterns of behaviour, carry out surveys to try to correlate possible cause and effect relations, build models and test new theories, all of which is in stark contrast to the paucity of kinds of investigations carried out in schools in the UK … Teachers see investigations as providing opportunities for pupils to make decisions, to think for themselves and to use scientific skills and processes to solve scientific problems, but do pupils see things in the same way? Do they have any idea of what they are supposed to be learning, or do they see investigations as just another school exercise to be done to keep the teacher happy?

Kinds of investigations

There are many different uses of the word 'investigations' in the literature … there was general agreement that:

- in investigative work pupils have to make their own decisions either individually or in groups: they are given some autonomy in how the investigation is carried out;
- an investigation must involve pupils in using investigational procedures such as planning, measuring, observing, analysing data and evaluating procedures. Not all investigations will allow pupils to use every kind of investigational procedure, and investigations may vary in the amount of autonomy given to pupils at different stages of the investigative process.

The model of investigative processes used in the National Curriculum (NC) has been based heavily on a structure in which students decide to change an independent variable, observe the effect on a dependent variable and control other key variables. This model is referred to in this chapter as the 'fair testing' model. This model has been softened in subsequent versions of the NC (such as DfE, 1995a) in order to accommodate a greater variety of approaches, but in spite of this the 'fair testing' model still dominates. The dominance of this model has led to the following problems:

- the investigations carried out in schools do not adequately represent the relationship between the development of scientific theories and empirical evidence;
- the variety of investigations used does not adequately represent the work that is carried out by scientists and presents a skewed picture of the nature of science;
- there is a tendency for some teachers to try to use fair testing procedures in investigations where they are not appropriate.

To help address these problems, a framework of six different kinds of investigations was proposed by the AKSIS project:

1. classifying and identifying: classification and identification of rocks;
2. fair testing: which paper towel soaks up most water?
3. pattern-seeking: do people with longer legs jump higher?
4. investigating models: how do optical illusions work?
5. exploring: what happens when different liquids are added together?
6. making things or developing systems: design a road bridge for a model car to cross.

Pupils' response to investigations

One characteristic that teachers feel is important in investigations is the amount of pupil autonomy. However, in a situation where more responsibility is given to pupils, it is important that they are clear about the educational purposes of what they are doing. Teachers' main justification for the inclusion of investigations in the science curriculum aim is to develop the use of the skills and processes of science (Watson and Wood-Robinson, 1998), with teaching for conceptual understanding taking second place. Another aim is to develop pupils' understanding of the relation between empirical data and scientific theory (Driver *et al.* 1996). The effectiveness of investigations for achieving these aims is discussed in Watson (2000).

Watson *et al.* (1998) compared teachers' aims for specific investigation lessons with what their pupils thought they learned. The mismatch between teacher and pupil perceptions is striking. About half the aims of the teachers were concerned with scientific procedures, with only a third of them being about learning content. Pupils, on the other hand, concentrated on more obvious features of investigations and so for about three quarters of the time saw the investigations as teaching them specific content, such as learning about dissolving. Only one fifth of their aims was about procedures, and again these tended to be very specific such as learning to operate a balance. A similar lack of clarity in understanding the aims was seen in a detailed observation study by Watson *et al.* (1999). The main focus of the lessons was in learning how to carry out fair testing procedures. The 12-year-old pupils were interviewed after the lessons:

Int: What do you think you've learned from doing your investigations?

R: That graph paper is stronger, that green one.

Int: Right. Is that it?

R: Um …

Int: You spent three lessons doing that, seems a long time to spend finding out that graph paper's stronger.

JA: Yeah … and we also found out which, um, paper's stronger. Not just the graph paper, all of them.

Many pupils approach the investigation as a routine exercise. They saw the worksheets as guiding them through set procedures and many seem to view satisfactory completion of the investigation as producing a set of completed worksheets.

Faced with such a lack of comprehension of the educational aims of an investigation, it is easy to see how teachers find it difficult to strike the balance between structuring an investigation to provide a framework for supporting students' thinking and structuring an investigation to drive pupils towards a predetermined outcome. Often teachers are unaware of how they are restricting pupils' choices, for example, by the way in which they introduce investigation or by the apparatus they provide (Watson and Wood-Robinson 1998). A useful way of analysing the balance between the decisions of the teacher and the pupils is to construct a decisions table. A decisions table for a visit to the zoo of a class of 8-year-old pupils is shown in Table 1.

Table 1 Decisions table for zoo visit

What to decide	What is decided	Who decides
How many similarities to observe	5	Teacher
How many differences to observe	5	Teacher
How many kinds of animals to observe	3	Teacher
Which animals	?	Pupils
What to record	?	Pupils
How many individuals of each kind to observe	?	Pupils
Which criteria are useful for constructing a key	?	Pupils after class discussion

The pupils were carrying out an investigation that involved them in classifying and identifying. They were using their observations of similarities and differences in order to decide what were good criteria to enable them to construct a key to identify a variety of animals. Before they went to the zoo, they had already had one lesson using pictures of animals to decide what characteristics to observe. The decisions table shows clearly where autonomy is given to the pupils. It also shows where the teacher may have to ask questions to support pupils' thinking (how will you decide which animals to observe? What will you be observing? What will you record?) and also where it is possible for the teacher to encroach on the pupils' autonomy and make the decisions for them instead of supporting their thinking.

Analysis

Watson *et al.* start by looking at how scientists carry out investigations and then use this as a model to look at teachers teaching science and children learning science. Interestingly and probably not surprisingly, they discover that the two groups hold different views about what is achieved when children undertake investigative work. The range of activities that make up scientific enquiry is possibly surprising, and points to the need for close scrutiny of schemes of work to ensure that children are offered these activities. Watson *et al.* raise a pertinent point when they explain that not all investigations will allow use of every kind of investigational procedure. This points to the fact that first you need to be able to analyse and be aware what opportunities each type of activity provides and to plan for a range of such activities over a period of time. The focus on children's autonomy is also an issue to be reflected on.

The findings that teachers lack comprehension of the educational aims of an investigation are possibly not surprising, particularly as there has been a reported lack of opportunity for most teachers to receive staff development in this area (OFSTED 2005), but it is difficult to understand that some teachers tend to use fair testing procedures in investigations when they are not appropriate. How, I wonder, does this operate in practice?

Watson *et al.*'s findings provide worrying reading, particularly in relation to the apparent lack of teacher awareness about what learning intentions are involved in investigational work, and the lack of understanding by children about what they are intended to learn. This suggests a lack of formative assessment at least when the extract was written and leads us, once again to ask if the described situation still is prevalent.

Of course, the examples provided in the six kinds of investigations are not exhaustive, and you will find that Goldsworthy (1998) provides more useful examples appropriate for the primary phase.

Personal response

Watson *et al.* paint a gloomy picture of the range of investigations undertaken in school. Compare this with your own experience of scientific enquiry in the primary classroom.

Why do you think teachers and children may hold different ideas about the purpose of scientific investigation?

Practical implications and activities

Working with a colleague:

- Make a note of the examples of activities linked to each of the six types of investigation identified and discussed in the extract and in the Goldsworthy reading.
- Consider a year group that is known to you. If you like, consult the QCA scheme of work for ideas then add further activities to those suggested in each category.
- Analyse a known scheme of work for the six types of investigation identified in the extract. Is there full coverage of these? Are there any gaps? If so, what are they and how can children's experience be enhanced in this area?
- Next time you plan a scientific investigation, use the decision table to aid your planning. How useful do you find the decision table presented in the extract? Is there a role for this sort of analysis at the planning stage?
- Goldsworthy (1998) suggests there are several things that you can do to help children engage with scientific method:

  - draw children's attention to different types of investigation and ensure that the teacher's questions match;
  - identify which decisions will be taken by children and which by the teacher;
  - teach children the skills and procedures of investigations, clarify how children can learn scientific procedures through doing and investigation (and explain this is the learning intention). Anticipate practical difficulties, particularly those related to measurement – provide good equipment with the appropriate degree of accuracy required by the task;
  - allow time to work with children to consider their evidence, using tables, bar charts and line graphs to explore patterns, make predictions and justify conclusions;
  - develop the language of investigations and teach children how to argue from evidence and challenge others' results;
  - use formative assessment to stimulate children to make progress in the skills and procedures of investigation.

Reflecting on your own planning and practice, to what extent do you plan for each of the above? Think about the planning and the implementation stage of your medium-term planning. Focus on children's learning during and immediately following the teaching. Evaluate the effectiveness of the strategies for children's learning and the extent to which you have been able to engage with this process.

Further reading

Goldsworthy, A and Feasey, R (1997) *Making sense of primary science investigations*. Hatfield: ASE.

5 Children's ideas

By the end of this chapter you should have:

- considered **why** children's ideas need to be explored at every stage of teaching;
- reflected upon **what** strategies can be used to develop children's scientific thinking;
- analysed **how** to take account of children's ideas in your own teaching.

Linking your learning

Sharp, J, Peacock, G, Johnsey, R, Simon, S, and Smith, R (2002) *Achieving QTS. Primary science: teaching theory and practice.* Chapter 4. Exeter: Learning Matters.

Professional Standards for QTS
2.4, 3.3.2, 3.3.6

Introduction

While emphasising the need for practical, hands-on exploration of the environment and the development of elements of scientific enquiry, this chapter will now consider the nature of children's ideas. As we saw in Chapter 1, science is important to children because it helps them to make sense of natural phenomena and, if presented in the right way, can be interesting and challenging. Although exploration and investigation are essential to the development of scientific ideas, illustrative and investigative activities will not, in themselves, necessarily lead to understanding. Undoubtedly children's ideas develop through practical exploration of their world, including ideas presented to them by their teachers. Based on research, the practice of eliciting children's ideas or 'starting where the children are' before teaching has long been advocated, but this has not always been the preferred approach. Numerous reasons have been advanced to explain why teachers fail to put this into practice. Building on Sharp *et al.*'s (2002) work, this chapter will consider further methods that you can use to develop children's ideas and understanding of science and will enable you to plan for work based on their ideas.

Research carried out over the last 20 years shows that children have very firmly-held ideas built up by their everyday experiences of the world. These unscientific ideas are called alternative frameworks or misconceptions and have a number of origins. Many arise where children wrongly apply ideas derived in one situation to another. Others stem from teaching in other disciplines, for example religious studies. These often conflict with the currently accepted views held by scientists and have been found to be very resistant to change by traditional, didactic teaching. Merely telling a child that their idea is incorrect and feeding the correct idea is unlikely to have any long-term effect. Instead, the child's idea needs to be confronted with science to support the new idea. Other misconceptions arise out of the ways we use everyday words that have specific meanings in science, e.g. 'animal', 'work', 'force', 'amphibian'. Others have their origin in what might be called old wives' tales. Whatever their origin, research tells us that these ideas need to be challenged through discussion and practical activity to enable the misconception to be confronted.

Sharp *et al.* (2002) provide an excellent summary of the main points involved in the development of ideas taken from the popular constructivist point of view, where children make sense of the world by constructing meaning from their everyday encounters with phenomena. You need to be aware that you can significantly influence children's ideas both for the better or the worse. It is particularly important that you do not teach science in a way that contributes to children's misconceptions. Unfortunately, it is very easy to do this unintentionally.

Why?

Why do children's ideas need to be explored at every stage of teaching?

Before you read the following extract, read:

- Harlen, W and Qualter, A (2004) 'Children's own ideas', chapter 2, in *The teaching of science in primary schools*. London: David Fulton.

Extract: Asoko, H (2002) 'Developing conceptual understanding in primary science', *Cambridge Journal of Education*, **Vol. 32 (2) pp153–164. London: Taylor & Francis Ltd.**

Learning science involves learning to use the ideas of science to interpret, explain and explore events and phenomena in the natural world. This is a long-term process which can be difficult. Misconceptions arise, knowledge may not be applied outside the classroom context and, even following instruction, learners may hold on to their original ideas. Research over the last 30 years has provided much information regarding children's thinking about natural phenomena … and knowledge change has been explored and interpreted from a range of perspectives.

Translating knowledge about learning into strategies for more effective teaching is, however, not straightforward … Teaching science involves stimulating a process of change in the thinking of the learner, but 'conceptual' change has to be viewed as a process of bewildering complexity, that is, dependent on many closely interrelated variables. These variables range from the classroom environment to the details of specific classroom interactions. Theoretical principles do not, therefore, translate unproblematically into context-specific teaching practices.

Teaching science concepts
Underpinning … [research studies about children's conceptual understanding] are a number of questions that can guide the planning of a piece of teaching. These are as follows:

1. What ideas and experiences do children have about this already? How are they likely to be thinking?
2. What exactly do I want children to understand or be able to do as a result of teaching?
3. What will happen 'in the learner's head' in moving from 1 to 2?
4. What teaching strategies might be used?
5. Which activities could be used? What would be the purpose of each? How could the learning opportunities be exploited?
6. How will this be managed in the classroom?

Points 1 and 2 define the anticipated starting points and end points of the learning. 'Starting from where the children are' and 'having clear learning objectives' are familiar phrases to teachers. However, here their importance is in considering the change which must happen 'in the learner's head' if learning is to occur. This involves recognition that it is not the children's ideas alone which are important, but the difference between these ideas and the science ideas to be taught.

Children's initial ideas may be used in teaching in different ways. Some teaching strategies require children's ideas to be made explicit then challenged in some way to stimulate learning. Alternatively, teaching approaches may focus on the ideas, which can be drawn upon and developed during the teaching. Challenging ideas may promote dissatisfaction with current thinking, which is seen to be as a prerequisite to, or driving force for, learning (Posner *et al.*, 1982). However, explicit elicitation of ideas in the classroom can be counter-productive. Children who feel that the ideas they put forward are always shown to be somehow inadequate may become demoralised and learn to keep their thoughts to themselves (Dreyfus *et al.*, 1990). Nevertheless some forms of puzzlement or surprise can engage interest and pave the way for new ideas. The teacher can then work to raise the status of some ideas at the expense of others (Hewson *et al.*, 1998).

Children may be receptive to considering a new idea, perhaps because they recognise that their current thinking is unsatisfactory or because their interest in a topic has been aroused in some way. However, if they are to make progress, they need new, and potentially better, ideas to change to. Deciding how and when an alternative way of thinking is to be introduced into the classroom is thus a crucial aspect of teaching for conceptual understanding. Scientific explanations draw upon ideas, which are human constructions. Although they arise from, and relate back to, experience, they are not directly obvious from it and so cannot be discovered by children through their own interactions with phenomena. Instead, children need to be introduced to, and helped to make sense of, new ways of describing and explaining that experience (Driver *et al.*, 1994a).

In primary schools much work involves broadening children's knowledge of phenomena and what affects them. Practical exploration can usefully contribute to this development. However, such activity also stimulates the need to explain observations and, in the absence of guidance, children will develop ideas, which seem to make sense to them. The teacher therefore needs to find ways to introduce and explain useful and relevant ideas at appropriate times and in ways that make sense to the children.

Discussion

Recognition of, and respect for, children's existing ideas has sometimes been interpreted as meaning that these should be explored at the start of every piece of teaching. Doing this might have several functions. Teachers might wish to check out assumptions about children's starting points, to 'cue children in' to the work or to refresh or reinforce their memory of earlier learning. It might be that explicit elicitation of ideas is necessary in order to stimulate learning. However, [in her research] neither teacher adopted this approach. That is not to say that they did not take account of children's thinking. Both were experienced teachers who had utilised information from relevant research sources and summaries ... this allowed them to anticipate what children would be likely to know and to use this information in planning how to introduce the new ideas on which they wished to focus.

Conclusion

Although primary science has made enormous advances over recent years, we know little about what children are capable of achieving in the most favourable conditions. Newton (1999) suggests that teachers value 'hands-on' activity but give little time to discourse which would support the development of understanding. Explaining is more than telling and can be difficult for teachers, especially if they do not themselves have a strong background in science. Going beyond simply labelling events and phenomena as examples of scientific ideas, towards making those ideas useful ways of thinking demands intellectual and creative effort on the part of both teachers and children. ... In the longer term, engaging and developing children's thinking more effectively means their understanding of and ability to apply the ideas of science must surely be enhanced.

Analysis

Research into children's ideas has a long history. Within the primary phase, SPACE (Scientific Processes and Concepts Exploration) research led to the development of influential curriculum materials for schools (Nuffield Primary Science). The starting point for both was the exploration of children's ideas as a basis for further work in the classroom. There is no doubt that research findings have influenced the way that some teachers approach science teaching, not least because Initial Teacher Training (ITT) and Continuing Professional Development (CPD) courses have emphasised this approach. Experience tell us, however, that this approach can be undeniably frightening for beginning teachers and those lacking in confidence about teaching science, so you might find this approach worrying and potentially difficult. Many experienced teachers, while claiming to base work on what children know, often find this more difficult in practice than in theory, and it is well known that many teachers will explore children's ideas and then proceed to follow a predetermined, prescribed route with no further account taken of the ideas children have raised.

Asoko's extract is very helpful because she offers an attractive alternative strategy to that involving an initial exploration of your children's ideas. She suggests that working *from* children's ideas can be very challenging but, given thorough preparation, working *with* children's ideas may be less so. In Asoko's model, there is still a clear need for teachers to know the misconceptions that children might hold in relation to a particular topic *before teaching*, so that if they arise they can be addressed through teaching.

This is a sensible suggestion because some children may genuinely not have any existing ideas about the science they encounter for the first time.

Alternatively, because children do not like to admit that they have no idea, and because they are highly creative, they may well make up a 'wrong' idea on the spur of the moment rather than not have an answer. In other words, the process of asking children a question may elicit a positive response to something that had never previously been considered. I have long suspected that asking children to provide an explanation, particularly if they are very young, might be counter-productive, because having articulated an idea that they have ownership of may well prove to be more attractive than the one the teacher wants to emerge. On the other hand, asking children what idea they have may well cause disappointment. For example, recently, some young children were asked to draw what they thought might be inside a seed prior to looking inside one. A number of ideas emerged, but the most popular was the idea that there was a miniature plant with all the parts such as stem, leaf, etc. all ready to emerge and get bigger when the seed was planted. On the one hand the children could be praised for their creative idea, but the difficulty came when the seed was cut open and children were disappointed because their ideas were wrong. This was particularly counter-productive because these children were disappointed when they should really have been struck by the awe and wonder at the germination of the seed. This exploration was further problematic because although some of the children's ideas were successfully challenged by discussion and practical activity, one child refused to accept the alternative view.

There is no doubt that young children have ideas of their own and these can be very creative. Here are some examples:

Q: Why does the moon shine?
A: Because the stars sprinkle light on it. (Girl, 5)

Q: What happens to leaves in the winter?
A: They fly away to Australia. (Boy, 5)

Q: Why are leaves green?
A: Because inside the tree, there is a syringe that puts green paint into the leaf. When the syringe is empty, the leaf turns brown. (Boy, 5)

Here are three very good examples of young children trying to make sense of aspects of their world, responding creatively to a question. It is easy to see how these answers might well be based on their experiences of literature mixed with other facts they might have had access to, for example, birds flying south for the winter.

In Asoko's model, children's ideas are not explored at the beginning of teaching. Rather, in her model of planning and implementation, flexibility is crucial. Unfortunately, this does not always sit comfortably with an activity-led, inflexible scheme of work where a particular rigid objectives model is followed. What you will need to do, if you adopt this approach, is to plan lessons and learning experiences that are sufficiently drafted in outline so that a flexible path can be woven through a previously well-explored area. The key factor here is that you need to anticipate what children would be likely to exhibit and use this information in planning how to introduce new ideas on which you need to focus.

Personal response

Think about your own approach to teaching science and the approaches that you have seen others use. To what extent do these:

- take account of children's prior ideas?
- explore children's ideas at each stage of teaching?
- adopt a flexible approach to planning?

Imagine that you have planned a lesson starting 'where the children are' followed by a pre-planned activity, only to find that the children's ideas bear no resemblance to those expected. How would you feel?

Practical implications and activities

Asoko's paper looked at how a different set of teaching methods could be used to challenge ideas as and when they arise in the ordinary course of teaching. At the planning stage teachers in her research identified:

- likely misconceptions children hold about the topic;
- science concepts to be introduced;
- activities that could be presented to children to support the development of their understanding of the science ideas – these provided a context and focus for ideas to be discussed, illustrated, explored and applied;
- ways that discussion can proceed.

She identified a number of factors that contributed to change in children's ideas:

- discussing the implications of children's existing knowledge;
- involving the children in seeking advice to support the new idea;
- highlighting a puzzle or contradiction to create a new model;
- using phenomena about which children could draw on a range of evidence to support predictions;
- helping children to make explicit the thinking behind correct predictions;
- introducing and exploring an analogy.

All activities, whether teacher-devised or adapted from published materials, had a specific purpose. They provided a context and focus for ideas to be discussed, illustrated, explored and applied. The role of the teacher was to stimulate and support children's thinking by posing problems, asking questions and modelling the use of new ideas.

Task
Research a topic to be taught, recording:

- the misconceptions highlighted by research;
- the accepted scientific idea;
- suitable activities to develop this idea.

Further reading

Johnsey, R, Peacock, G, Sharp, J and Wright, D (2002) *Achieving QTS. Primary science: knowledge and understanding* (2nd edn.) Exeter: Learning Matters.

Wenham, M (2004) *Understanding primary science.* London: PCP.

These texts will help you to identify the accepted scientific understanding that you will need to teach specific science topics in the primary classroom. Dip into them when you are planning to teach a specific topic.

What?

What strategies can be used to develop children's scientific thinking?

Before you read the following extract, read:

- Galton, M (2002) 'Continuity and progression in science teaching at Key Stages 2 and 3', *Cambridge Journal of Education*, 32, (2).

Extract: Mercer, N, Dawes, L, Wegerif, R, Sams, C (2004) 'Reasoning as a scientist: ways of helping children to use language to learn science', *British Educational Research Journal*, 30 (3) pp359-77. London: Taylor & Francis Ltd.

Educational researchers who adopt a sociocultural perspective have commonly depicted science education as a discursive process, whereby novices (students) are inducted into a way of representing and understanding phenomena (using language and other representational means) by those more expert in the field … Contemporary sociocultural theorists … follow Vygotsky (e.g. 1978) in emphasising the importance of language use and social interaction within communities for the development of educated ways of making sense of the world, such as those associated with science … To the best of our knowledge no direct relation has been demonstrated between encouraging students to engage in certain ways of using spoken language and their improved understanding or attainment in science. One group of studies has shown that discussion can contribute to the development of conceptual understanding in science (Howe *et al.*, 2000), but that research did not encourage the pragmatic use of particular forms of dialogue … Their findings provide support for the value of discussion and investigation by children without the authoritative presence of a teacher, while also showing that expert involvement can have a crucial and beneficial influence for guiding children's activity in productive directions.

One link between the learning of science and the use of language is the development of a specialised vocabulary for representing concepts and describing processes. In addition, spoken language provides a familiar medium through which a child can describe their conceptions of phenomena in order that teachers assess a level of understanding (Ollerenshaw and Ritchie, 1998).

There are two main contexts in which spoken language can be related to the learning of science in schools. The first is teacher-led interaction with pupils. … The second context is that of peer group interaction. Working in pairs or groups, children are involved in interactions which are more 'symmetrical' than those of teacher-pupil discourse and so have different kinds of opportunities for developing reasoned arguments, describing observed events, etc. In science education, such collaboration can be focused on practical investigations, which also have great potential value for helping children to relate their developing understanding of abstract ideas to the physical world.

A possible explanation for the doubtful quality of much collaborative talk is that children do not bring to this task a clear conception of what they are expected to do, or what would constitute a good, effective discussion. This is not surprising as many children may rarely encounter examples of such discussion in their lives out of school – and teachers rarely make their own expectations or criteria for effective discussion explicit to children (Mercer, 1995). Children are rarely offered guidance or training in how to communicate effectively in groups. Even when the aim of talk is made explicit … there may be no real understanding of how to talk together or for what purpose. … On this basis, we began this research with the hypothesis that children studying science would benefit from teacher guidance of two main kinds. First … they need to be helped to gain relevant knowledge of natural phenomena, investigative procedures, scientific concepts and terms – the content of science. Teachers commonly do provide this guidance. Second, they need to be helped to learn how to use language to enquire, reason, and consider information together, to share and to negotiate their ideas, and to make joint decisions.

The intervention programme

… A key feature of the 'Thinking Together' programme was the systematic integration of teacher-led interaction and group-based interaction. … More specifically, the programme was intended to ensure that children became able to carry out the kind of discussion we call Exploratory Talk. This is talk in which:

- all relevant information is shared;
- all members of the group are invited to contribute to the discussion;
- opinions and ideas are respected and considered;
- everyone is asked to make their reasons clear;
- challenges and alternatives are made explicit and are negotiated;
- the group seeks to reach agreement before taking a decision or acting.

Each teacher was provided with 12 detailed lesson plans. These lessons involved a teacher-led introduction, a group discussion activity, and a final 'sharing' plenary session. The aims of the lesson were to do with the teaching and learning of explicit talk skills such as critical questioning, sharing information, or negotiating a decision. The first five lessons were aimed at raising children's awareness of how talk could be used for working together and establishing in each class a set of 'ground rules' for discussion which would generate talk of an exploratory talk. The further seven lessons encouraged children to apply their developing discussion skills to the study of the science … curriculum for Year 5. Each lesson applied a specific talk skill and targeted a specific concept in science.

Discussion and conclusions

The research … demonstrated that an experimental teaching programme enabled children in primary schools to work together more effectively, improve their language and reasoning skills and reach higher levels of attainment in their study of science. … By showing that children's increased use of certain ways of using language leads to better learning and conceptual understanding in science, we have provided empirical support for the conception of science education as induction into a community of discourse or practice … Our findings therefore add to the evidence that the development of scientific understanding is best assisted by a careful combination of peer group interaction and expert guidance, and provide an example of how that combination can be successfully achieved.

… The teachers in the project schools have created talk-focused classrooms in which the children … are each other's resource. But this does not mean that teachers abdicated responsibility for guiding the construction of knowledge; their role in enabling children to gain a better understanding of interpersonal communication and curriculum content was crucial. … More confident children gain the opportunity to hear a wider range of views. Quieter children find that their contribution is sincerely requested and valued. One of the simplest but most profound benefits for children is the idea that challenging each other is not just accepted, but encouraged. … Our findings indicate that if teachers provide children with an explicit, practical introduction to the use of language for collective reasoning then children learn better ways of thinking collectively and better ways of thinking alone.

Analysis

In this extract, Mercer *et al.* highlight the need to have a cross-curricular approach to teaching science and emphasise the importance of effective group work in the development of children's ideas. This fits well with the current move in primary education. Group work has long been advocated in primary science as a means of sharing ideas, particularly in relation to practical work. However, in Galton's original work on the ORACLE project, he found that although many teachers advocated group work this was often characterised by children grouped together while working on individual tasks. Grouping was rarely used productively to facilitate collaborative learning. As we saw in Chapter 2, in his most recent research Galton (2002) reported on too much whole-class teaching and less experimentation than was desirable in Year 6. Clearly, this is not a situation that is likely to promote the positive aspects of language development, reasoning skills and children's understanding of scientific ideas in the way that Mercer *et al.* (2004) suggest is possible. Furthermore, Galton's most recent findings suggest that group work is often underused or dominated by one child.

Mercer's view is that in addition to providing opportunities for children to acquire the 'content of science' they also need to learn how to consider arguments, share and negotiate ideas and make joint decisions. This is important because, in doing so, they will not only develop their understanding and develop the links between aspects of science (sometimes referred to as the 'big ideas' in science) but will also develop the generic skills needed for the development of the science-literate individual. These generic skills are needed by individuals working in teams and are also very important for the articulation and development of scientific understanding. It is well known that ideas produced as a result of joint exploration can far exceed the ideas of one person working alone. Furthermore, peer group interaction, joint study, exploration and argument can challenge ideas in a far less threatening way than challenge initiated by the teacher.

In your teaching, you will frequently meet children who hold a range of misconceptions. In order for their ideas to meet those accepted by the wider scientific community, they need to be challenged, for example, by undertaking practical activities or through the use of an analogy or a model that can help children to understand complex scientific ideas. This provides the opportunity for new ideas to be explored and adopted. However, many children, even those who might be thought too young to be able to think about ideas in the abstract, can change their ideas through discussion, or a combination of discussion and practical activity, particularly discussion with their peers. Practical activities are important because, as Sharp *et al.* tell us, they lay the foundations for an understanding of major scientific ideas at a later stage, and you also need to highlight the scientific knowledge and understanding implicit in the activities. This aspect of teaching is often not planned for or evident in practice.

Personal response

- To what extent do you allow the children to explore and explain their ideas to yourself and their peers?
- To what extent do you use group work in your teaching?
- Do you explain how children can discuss together in the way Mercer describes?

Practical implications and activities

The approach advocated in the extract involves a high level of organisation for group work. Teachers often find this threatening or difficult to manage. Difficulties often arise because children are not used to working in this way, or the group size is too big (see Chapter 6).

- If your children are not used to group work, try putting them into pairs or threes for discussion, followed by an opportunity for the pairs to report back to the class on their ideas. Ideas can then be collated and individual ideas discussed within a whole class plenary. This is an opportunity for children to ask further questions about individual ideas, for further explanations to be given and for some ideas to be challenged.
- Ask children initially to work in pairs to explore ideas, then put two pairs together to share ideas, as above.

It is important to emphasise that it is the idea that is to be challenged, not the children who have expressed the ideas.

- Work with one group (or ask a teaching assistant to work with a group and to record the results). Your role is to listen to the group discussion without comment. You could explain that you are recording their ideas for discussion afterwards. Make a careful note of what is said, then analyse the interaction as follows:

– How many different ideas were generated?
– Did the children challenge any of the ideas? If so, which and how were they challenged?
– Did the ideas of the group change as a result?

Record any interesting examples.

Further reading

Blake, A (2004) 'Helping young children to see what is relevant and why: supporting cognitive change in earth science using analogy', *International Journal of Science Education*, 26, (15) pp. 1855–1873.

Harlen, W and Qualter, A (2004) 'Ways of helping the development of ideas', chapter 9 in *The teaching of science in primary schools,* London: David Fulton.

How?

How can you take account of children's ideas in your own teaching?

Before you read the following extract, record:

• what is meant by causal understanding in science and how this can be fostered.

Extract: Newton, P D and Newton, L D (2000) 'Do teachers support causal understanding through their discourse when teaching primary science?', *British Educational Research Journal*, 26 (5). London: Taylor & Francis Ltd.

Understanding is worthwhile. It can make responses flexible, facilitate further learning, and is often durable and satisfying. Furthermore, at a time when information is cheap and abundant, making sense of it is likely to be what matters (Shenk, 1997). This does not mean that those who understand always perform better, but they tend to learn more quickly and are more able to apply that learning in novel situations (Winkles, 1986; Minnaert and Janssen, 1992; Hiebert and Wearne, 1996).

In science, understanding is 'the connecting of facts, the relating of newly acquired information to what is already known, the weaving of bits of knowledge into an integrated and cohesive whole'. It often involves finding a unifying principle or mentally connecting cause and effect (Nickerson, 1985; Sierpinska, 1994). This connecting relating and weaving may be directed towards a variety of mental ends, as in grasping concepts (such as circuit and series), understanding descriptions of situations, events or procedures (such as the sequence in the life cycle of a butterfly and how to use a classification key), and understanding causes of events and reasons for procedures (such as why mosses tend to grow on the north side of tree trunks and why sieves should be used in a particular sequence when filtrates are to be separated by size) (Newton, 1996, 2000). Such mental connections may exist below the level of consciousness (Claxton, 1997), but Brown (1997) sees 'the most stringent [criterion] of understanding [as involving] the availability of knowledge to conscious reflection'. Further, Piaget (1978) felt that only those mental structures that answered the question 'why' deserve to be called understanding and these can figure in science a lot of the time. Certainly, attaining a conscious causal understanding of a situation is the aim of much scientific endeavour (Emmet, 1985; Kitcher and Salmon, 1989; Solymar, 1999). Given that, it is not surprising that causal understanding is an acknowledged goal of science teaching (see for example, Scottish Office for Education, 1993; DfEE, 1995) and trainee teachers in England and Wales must be taught to make such understandings explicit in their lessons (DfEE, 1988).

However, understanding cannot be transmitted from teacher to child. Children must make mental connections for themselves but the process can be supported. The capacity to construct an inference, the basis of understanding, is thought to be innate (Caine and Caine, 1994; Premack and Premack, 1995). There is evidence that children as young as three years old can link events causally (Dunn and Brown, 1993). Newton tested 5–11-year-olds' ability to understand scientific cause and effect and concluded that they generally could do so in the learning contexts commonly found in the primary school (Newton, 1996). The sophistication of the inference, however, develops with age.

In science, not just any mental connection will do; what counts is usually what is at least on the way to being acceptable to the scientific community. In striving towards this end, teachers' efforts are sometimes frustrated by children's existing mental frameworks.

In a study of primary education, Her Majesty's Inspectorate (HMI) identified 'a high level of interaction' between teacher and pupils as a feature of lessons with 'high standards of achievement'. This interaction included discourse which exhibits 'good questioning skills' … 'The most effective teaching makes use of discussion and probing questions to encourage pupils to … develop understanding' (Ofsted, 1999). More than that, there is strong experimental evidence that discourse in primary science which focuses on relationships, causes and reasons can promote causal understanding. … [Q]uestions that target these can provide effective support for such an understanding … requiring learners to make predictions is known to support the construction of coherent mental representations of situations … Providing conceptual structures and explaining have also been shown to be able to support the construction of coherent mental structures … On the other hand, discourse that is largely descriptive and factual tends to generate mental structures that cluster facts rather than relate new ideas and facts in explanatory structures.

The point is that the construction of conscious, causal understanding can be fostered by discourse to do with causal connections and relationships. Gallos (1995) believes that the development of understanding in science is, essentially, a language task … furthered by guided, didactic conversation. … [C]lassroom discourse to do with drawing inferences, giving reasons and integrating information depends more on the teacher than the child.

Understanding, however, may not be a priority in the classroom … often what counts is facility in reproducing information. … In Scotland, Harlen and Holroyd (1997) found that teachers who lack confidence in teaching science cope by teaching it as little as possible, by stressing process rather than conceptual development, by relying on activity and text, and by underplaying questioning and discussion. If a teacher shrinks from causal discourse then children may fail to see causal understanding as a goal in science and favour description and the acquisition of information. … Why might causal understanding be neglected?

Discussion and conclusions

… The aim of the study was to gauge the extent to which primary teachers press for causal understanding in their oral discourse in science lessons. It was found that teachers' discourse was often largely confined to developing vocabulary and descriptive understandings of phenomena and situations. Often, there was little evidence of an oral press for causal understanding, with its persistent emphasis on reasoning, argument and explanation. The teachers who gave least time to causal questioning in their oral discourse also tended to be amongst those who did not provide a practical activity. This suggests that the lack of an oral press for causal understanding may not always be made good through practical work. In any event, unsupported practical activity is not a certain way to understanding. The other activities presented here were often directed towards vocabulary development and description rather than cause and effect.

Analysis

Duggan and Gott (2002) argued for science education to focus more on the development of children's procedural understanding than is currently the case and, because of the need to develop a more scientifically literate society, there should be more emphasis on children's understanding of science rather than transitory memorising of facts. Their argument was that tomorrow's citizens need to be able to weigh up arguments and recognise when information is reliable and valid. That view is reinforced when Newton and Newton commented it is easy to access a whole range of information, but making sense of that information is what is important to the individual. They also indicate that those who can apply their learning in a novel situation are likely to be more creative. Creativity in science needs to be fostered with more emphasis placed on developing understanding.

These are useful pointers for teachers to promote causal understanding. Importantly, you must value understanding and devote time to it in your teaching. You need to explore children's understanding and press them to explain their understanding, support and develop it. This relates back to the first extract in this chapter, which suggests that you need to know both what misconceptions you might encounter, and what the more accepted scientific idea would be so that children can be guided by practical activity and discussion.

Personal response

Reflect on your own teaching. To what extent do you:

- ask children to explain why they have arrived at an idea or a conclusion in your teaching?
- promote understanding rather than emphasising recall of facts?
- give understanding priority over other aspects of teaching?
- provide opportunities for children to record information?

Practical implications and activities

Many teachers argue that there is not enough time available to allow children to discuss their ideas but it is essential that opportunities are provided to do so. When planning, it is important that you set aside time within individual lessons to provide these opportunities.

With a colleague, analyse your teaching using the following observation schedule. Record the number of times you engage with each behaviour listed below.

Aspect of teaching	Frequency of action									
Children discuss their ideas together										
Children provide factual answer by recall										
Child explains answer										
Child justifies answer										
You recognise a correct answer										
Children record information in some way										
Child disagrees with another										
Child appears to change ideas										

Reflect on this information. What other aspects of teaching and learning in science could you include in your analysis? What action needs to be taken?

Further reading

Pine, K, Messer, D and St John, K (2001) 'Children's misconceptions in primary science: a survey of teachers' views'. *Research in Science and Technological Education*, 19 (1).

6 Grouping children for science

By the end of this chapter you should have:

- considered **why** it is unusual to group children by ability in science;
- reflected on **what** research can tell us about single gender grouping in science;
- analysed **how** peer and parent tutoring can assist learning of science.

Linking your learning

Sharp, J, Peacock, G, Johnsey, R, Simon, S, and Smith, R. (2002) *Achieving QTS: Primary science: teaching theory and practice.* Exeter: Learning Matters.

Professional Standards for QTS
1.7, 3.3.2, 3.3.3, 3.3.4, 3.3.6, 3.3.7, 3.3.12

Introduction

There is no doubt that the social and educational groups to which an individual belongs can have long-term effects on life chances. School groupings have been of interest to researchers for many years and have focused on both macro and micro levels. Early research into streaming (an early form of grouping), in grammar and secondary modern schools by Hargreaves (1967) and Lacey (1970) contributed to the equal opportunities debate which led to the reorganisation of secondary education in many parts of the UK. Certainly, the resulting comprehensive education provided more opportunity for children from a wider variety of backgrounds than ever before. At primary level, change was not so radical because many primary schools were usually not big enough to support streaming. Instead, setting by ability within a class was more the norm and as Hallam (2003, 2004) reports, continues to operate today.

Evidence from a range of sources suggests that grouping at the micro level can also have a significant effect on children. Many texts have considered how to group children within the class, but then fail to advise on how the groups should be made up. There are also disagreements between writers on group size. Harlen and Qualter (2004, p206) say that groups of four are ideal, but suggest that 8–12-year-olds can be in groups as large as six although smaller numbers are desirable. On the other hand, Sharp *et al.* (2002, p73) report that it is common for teachers to have four or five groups each with between 6–8 children in science. Ward (2005, p144) however, suggests that different activities require different groupings, so individual work, paired work, or groups of four are suitable for different purposes. Groups of more than four rarely work unless the focus is on discussion or drama because of the limited number of roles possible.

Grouping by ability has always been popular. Like all groupings, ability groups have their advantages and disadvantages. It is said that differentiation is easier by ability groups. Setting children and grouping by ability within classes has been advocated and practised in a belief that it will increase attainment and raise standards. In primary education as in higher education, children often remain with the same 'class' group from year to year, sometimes not having the opportunity to know older, or younger children let alone work with them. Working with the same group of children or trainees can be comfortable, predictable, and 'safe' for both teacher and child. Yet, this may not provide the challenge that is really needed to prepare children, or for that matter trainees, for their future role in society.

There are other kinds of grouping that are worthy of examination and therefore this chapter will provide the opportunity for reflection on these. In fact the whole area of grouping children is ripe for investigation at a class level, but is fraught with difficulty because of the complex nature of possible variations resulting from the complex nature of interaction within groups. There are so many factors involved and too many variables, therefore any research into the effect of different grouping is far from straightforward, but potentially very interesting. This chapter looks at some interesting perspectives on grouping children in science.

Why?

Why is it unusual for children to be grouped by ability in science?

Reflect on your own personal experience of grouping children for science:

- were these groupings effective?
- if yes, why and for what purpose?

Try to find the assumptions about children working in groups that underpin the observed practice.

Before you read the following extract, read:

- Hallam, S, Ireson, J and Davies, J (2004) 'Primary pupils' experiences of different types of grouping in school', *British Educational Research Journal* 30 (4).
- Hallam, S, Ireson, J, Lister, V and Chaudhury, I A (2003) 'Ability grouping practices in the primary school: a survey'. *British Educational Research Journal,* 29 (1).

Extract: Qualter, A (1996) 'Grouping in science', *Differentiated primary science,* **pp19–20. Buckingham: Open University Press.**

Grouping in science
Recently I asked a group of teacher training students, who were spending time observing in different primary schools, to find out how teachers group for science. Not one of the 53 students saw children grouped by ability for science. This matches the findings of larger studies, which note that children tend to work in groups according to reading ability, or English or maths performance. In my own experience of visiting many

classes, seating tends to be by some measure of general ability, or teachers encourage children to sit in friendship groups. With the introduction of the National Curriculum and its associated assessment arrangements, teachers are tending more towards grouping by 'ability'. Yet at the same time teachers often say that a child whose reading ability or mathematical skills are not so good can come into his or her own in science. It is worth asking the question of whether it is appropriate to use maths or language performance as a measure of general ability, or of ability in science. Sally and Mike Willson looked at children's scores on maths and English standard tests, and on NFER reading tests. They compared these scores with pupils' performance on the knowledge and understanding of science (Attainment Targets 2, 3 and 4 of the science curriculum) and found no correlation between any of the scores and performance on the knowledge and understanding of science tests. Interestingly, however, perfomance on the first attainment target (investigations) did correlate with scores on the English, maths and reading tests (see Table).

The relationship between performance of pupils in different aspects of the curriculum (correlation coefficients for 30 children)

	English	Maths	Reading
Science (overall)	0.40	0.28	0.22
PC1 (investigations)	0.60a	0.71 [a]	0.51 [a]
PC2 (content knowledge)	0.44	0.24	0.23

[a] significant correlations

Source: Willson and Willson (1994 p15)

There are many reasons why teachers place children in fixed groups for much of the time within the classroom. Many use some form of integrated day. One group might be working on language tasks while another is doing a science investigation, and another is working through a maths book. This allows teachers to make the best use of scarce resources. The most valuable of these is the teacher's time. If one group is working on an activity that needs little teacher attention, the teacher is released to work with another group whose demands are higher. Children also get used to working with the others in their group and are more relaxed and happy as a result. Yet the temptation is to see the members of any one group as homogeneous in terms of their ability in all areas. I doubt if any teacher would agree that this is the case with any group in a class. The problem remains that teachers need to be able to provide each child with opportunities to learn that are appropriate to that child.

As part of a research project to evaluate the implementation of science in the National Curriculum, a large sample of teachers from across England was interviewed about teaching science (Russell et al. 1994). Many of these teachers raised their concerns about judging ability in science. Teachers often cited the child who in most situations is considered less able, but who shows real ability in science:

> I have a boy in my less able group, his reading and writing are not good at all; but in science he really shines. He has lots of ideas and can think of ways to test them.

> The trouble is he falls down on recording, so I can't give him the higher levels, because I know he won't do so well in the tests.
>
> The individual children mentioned so often in discussion highlight a dilemma for teachers that goes beyond concern about individuals. The fact that these children seem to be bringing something to science lessons that is not required by other subjects raises a number of questions about what is valued in the science curriculum, and what skills, knowledge and understanding are appropriately brought to science learning by children. The question then is: what makes science special or important in the education of children? What does it contribute in particular to their general education?

Analysis

Given that the grouping might have a significant effect on children's learning in science, questions must be asked about the most effective grouping arrangement for optimum learning to occur. However, it is difficult to determine this as little or no comparative research is available to inform our practice. Qualter suggests that many teachers use same groupings as for English and maths and puts forward reasons for this. Does this practice continue today and what are the underpinning assumptions that teachers make in grouping for teaching science? What is the most common grouping found for science today? This question may be difficult to answer because our personal experience may be limited. Is it based on ability, or mixed ability or some other grouping, for example, friendship grouping? What does research tell us?

In primary schools where setting by ability was common, Hallam (2003, p74) reported very little setting in science compared with English and mathematics and a high incidence of the use of mixed ability groups. If setting and grouping by ability is the recommended strategy for raising attainment in primary schools, why is it not common practice in science? This raises the question of why science is not treated like English and mathematics. Is it that the nature of science is fundamentally different to these core subjects and, therefore, requires different practice, or is it that teachers find it hard to assess children in science and therefore take the easy option of using mixed ability grouping? What is the rationale and justification for grouping in this manner or an alternative preferred manner? Why do some teachers adopt friendship groups?

If children remain in the same groups for English or mathematics is the assumption that their ability is the same in science, could it be laziness on the part of the teacher, or something else? Complex questions like these are difficult to answer and potentially relatively difficult to research, but they are pertinent questions and deserve to be raised and explored. What are the assumptions that underpin grouping practice? Is there a tendency for children to remain in the same groups all day, all week? If so why? Are there any other considerations that are particular to science? Do those children labelled as 'less able' in English or maths sometimes 'shine' in science? If so, what could be the reason for this? If grouping by ability benefits children in English and mathematics then it is not unreasonable to assume that this would be so for science too. If we were to group by ability in science, what would we use as a measure of ability? Qualter presents some quantitative data. What does this tell us? What might be the reasons for these findings? Would it be possible to investigate the relationship between performance in English and mathematics at the class level and, if so, what data could be collected and how could it be analysed?

Personal response

- Do you prefer to use friendships groups when you teach, if so why? Do you use the same groupings for English or mathematics, if so, why? Or, do you use ability groups? If so, how do you decide on your groupings?
- What are the assumptions about children's learning in science that underpins your preferred grouping for science?
- Make a note of these. Is there a pattern? What conclusions do you draw from your analysis of your own teaching in this area?

Practical implications and activities

- Talk to a more experienced teacher about grouping. Find out if there has been any change in relation to grouping children for science. What change, if any, has there been and what has driven the change?
- Share your reflections with a colleague. Do you share the same understanding as others or are your views different? Is there a whole-school policy on grouping?
- Consider some individual children and their ability in science. Compare the examples of work collected to support your assessment of them in English, mathematics and science. What do you notice?
- Look again at the examples of work collected for science. On what are you judging your children's performance? Look for evidence relating to skills, concepts and attitudes in science. Can you draw any conclusions about ability in science from your children's work?

Further reading

Watt, D (2002) 'Assisting performance: a case study from a primary classroom'. *Cambridge Journal of Education*, 32 (2).

Ireson, J, and Hallam, S (1999) 'Raising standards: is ability grouping the answer?' *Oxford Review of Education*, 25 (3).

What?

What can research tell us about single-gender grouping in science?

Before you read the following extract, read:

- Ward, H (2005) 'Organisational issues', chapter 10, pp143–145 in Ward, H, Roden, J, Hewlett, C, and Foreman, J, *Teaching science in the primary classroom: a practical guide.* London: Paul Chapman Publishing.

Extract: Robinson, W P (2004) 'Single-sex teaching and achievement in science', *International Journal of Science Education,* **14 May 2004, 26 (6), pp660–661 and 666– 667. London: Taylor & Francis Ltd.**

Arguments put forward to explain the changes in gender differences in attainment that have examined school-related factors have focused severally on changes in the curriculum, assessment processes, pedagogy, and pupil attitudes and behaviour. Studies have found that girls have more positive attitudes than boys towards school and learning (Arnot *et al.,* 1998; Office for Standards in Education and Equal Opportunities Commission, 1996; Warrington and Younger, 1997). They are more attentive in class and more willing to do extra work and homework; they tend to underestimate their ability and work harder to compensate, in contrast to boys, who are more likely to be over-confident and to over-estimate their ability (Office for Standards in Education and Equal Opportunities Commission 1996; Pickering 1997; Warrington and Younger, 1997).

The concern about the relatively lower achievement of boys has been expressed in educational policy initiatives at national, local and school levels. Several different types of strategies have been implemented within schools (Sukhandan, 1999). These have targeted both boys and girls, although the proportion of interventions specifically targeting boys has increased in the past few years. The strategies adopted at the school level tend to focus on classroom organisation practices and teaching methods, with a switch to single-sex (SS) classes as being one of the more commonly adopted forms of intervention. The idea of arranging for SS classes in mixed-sex schools was in part based on a particular interpretation of the relatively prominent positions of all-girl schools' published performance school league tables. These have reinforced the belief that girls would do better in SS classes and may imply the same would be true for boys. Recent research, however, suggests that factors of ability, social class, and the history and tradition of all-girls' schools, have much greater impact on girls' academic performance than SS education *per se* (Hannan *et al.,* 1996; Daly 1996; Robinson and Smithers, 1999). Historically, a switch to SS in science and mathematics has been targeted at girls, whereas SS classes aimed at boys have been adopted in subjects such as modern foreign languages and English, where the reverse gender performance gaps were greatest. Researchers urge caution in interpreting the findings of evaluation studies in this area; on occasions experimental periods may have been too short to assess potential benefits, and other variables may be difficult to control (Arnot *et al.,* 1998). Harvey (1985) reported that SS groups in science in the first year of secondary schooling did not improve girls' attainment, and in a later study Harvey and Stables (1986) suggested that SS classes might help to change stereotyped gendered attitudes towards subjects.

Attitudes of pupils to SS teaching itself may also be relevant. Kenway (1995) reported that boys in SS mathematics classes were noisier in the classroom, spent less time on tasks, and complained that they missed the girls helping them with work. According to Crump (1990) (quoted in Arnot *et al.,* 1998), boys put into SS science classes showed 'a lingering resentment and lesser ability to cope with the change than girls'. In contrast to these results, the National Foundation for Educational Research (NFER) (Sukhandan *et al.*, 2000) study found boys viewed SS classes positively. They reported being more interested and motivated in their work and that the absence of girls helped improve their confidence and their level of involvement in lessons. Girls tended to be less convinced of either the academic or the social impact of these classes. Explanations for these different findings may be associated with the fact that in the NFER study SS classes were explicitly implemented to improve boys' achievement, and girls may have felt resentful of the schools' emphasis on boys as a consequence (pp660–661).

Qualitative data

1. Teachers' comments. The practicalities of timetabling resulted in two women and one man having all-girl classes, and two men and two women having all-boy classes. Teachers of the lower sets commented on the wide range of ability in their classes and the impact of this on their teaching; this was especially true for those teaching boys where two classes had a high proportion of pupils with special educational needs (SEN). The diversity of competence amongst the LS boys was said to have slowed down class progress, even with additional teacher support provided for SEN pupils … LS girls presented different difficulties for the teachers: too much chatter, too much out-of-turn commentary, too many demands for instant teacher help.

Both teachers of HS classes thought their classes had made greater progress in the SS classes than previous cohorts had in mixed ones. The teacher of the HS girls remarked how much more constructive and task-oriented they were on their own. There was much less chatter. They worked co-operatively in small groups, sharing equipment, answering questions without interruption. The teacher of the HS boys thought that they had participated with greater confidence in general class discussions, although during small-group practical work they had not concentrated so well, particularly when this involved written tasks. With the exception of one teacher of one LS girls class, all the other teachers of both HS and LS classes reported good rapport with their groups and commented on enhanced confidence of HS and LS boys and girls in asking and answering questions, and on the absence of inter-sex related interruptions.

2. Pupils' comments. Two main themes dominated the group discussions, one related to doing science constructively and the other to social interaction. First regarding doing science well and constructively, the wish to work and being able to do so were seen to be more easily realised in SS classes. Such comments were much commoner in HS groups and were expressed most strongly by HS girls. In particular, HS girls viewed science lessons as serious opportunities for learning. They were keen to do well in GCSE. While they regretted the loss of the positive interactions with boys in mixed classes, they felt this loss was more than compensated for.

Girls' comments:

It's a bit boring and less fun in a single sex group, but its faster moving, you don't have as many people being told off and you definitely learn more.

I think without boys there's less of a laugh but no distraction. Last year I was always sitting next to two people who messed about most of the time.

Last year the boys were very clever, and I felt stupid asking questions. This year it's easier, and we explain it to each other.

The HS boys also wanted to do well, but in contrast to the girls did not think their progress in science had been compromised previously in mixed sex classes. They reported feeling more confident in a class without girls though they missed the 'service' role provided by girls in mixed classes.

Boys' comments:

With boys I feel more confident, but I prefer it with girls.

With not having mixed groups you might ask the teacher specific things 'cos you don't have to worry about the girls. They did help me in the practicals though.

You say things you wouldn't say in front of the girls, but this means there's more shouting out. With the girls we used to get down to work right away.

The boys thought progress in their work was compatible within their customary time commitments.

LS boys and girls were much less likely to mention motivation to do well as a basis for their preference for mixed or single-sex classes.

Second, regarding social interaction the enjoyment of social activity alongside learning dominated the arguments in favour of mixed classes, and these were advanced most by LS pupils and by girls in particular. It was the loss of possibilities of having a bit of fun and chat with the other sex that was missed. Pupils viewed this as 'being deprived' and cited SS teaching as 'unnatural' and therefore undesirable.

Boys' comments:

You miss out on girls' company; you don't get as big a range of opinions.

Girls are altogether more calm; I am more easy to distract if they aren't there.

Boys on their own can be mad and loopy sometimes.

Girls' comments

Girls on their own can be boring.

I think without boys girls can get very bitchy and gossipy and it isn't as much fun when there's no one to fancy.

Seems strange without boys, and you don't have a laugh when they give stupid answers.

There was no mention of resentment at the experiment, but a clear preference was expressed for a reversion to mixed classes in Year 10 among LS pupils.

Analysis

This interesting extract was based on research into a whole-year group of 13-year-old children in an urban Church of England secondary school, and relates to single-sex classes rather than gender groupings within a class. At first glance, the extract may be dismissed as not providing anything of value to the primary sector, but are there differences between girls and boys at the primary level, and, if so, are the differences similar to or different from those in the extract? Are there implications here for the grouping of children in science in the primary school that needs to be taken account of at the planning stage?

Experience and close observation of children's interaction in class at the primary level suggest that there are some significant gender differences in girls' and boys' approach to learning and, in particular to practical activities in primary science. Boys have been described as 'hunter-gatherers' when collecting and using science equipment while girls have a tendency to plan more carefully, talk more about tasks to be undertaken and often take particular roles like recording data.

There are a number of investigative questions that could be raised. For example, if there are differences, would it be better to have single or mixed gender groupings? If boys do tend to dominate practical science activities, would it be better for girls to work in single-sex groupings? Alternatively, if boys tend not to think about what they are going to do, and do not take on particular roles in group work, would boys be better in single gender groups? What are the advantages of mixed gender groups? Do girls prefer to work with girls or boys? Do boys prefer mixed or single gender groups? Such a complex area requires careful consideration, especially in relation to reliability, validity and the extent to which findings in any one context can be generalised to the larger population.

The research reported in the extract was relatively large-scale involving a whole year group. It drew upon a range of both quantitative and qualitative data collected and analysed as evidence. The use of quantitative data is often said to provide more objective evidence, while qualitative evidence provides different insights and can illuminate quantitative data. In practice, collecting a range of evidence in this way can increase the validity and reliability of the findings. After analysing the collected data, the concluding suggestion was that single-sex teaching offered affordable benefits for pupils and that mixed-sex teaching had specific disadvantages. Despite this, the result of the research was that the school returned to mixed-sex groups in the following year. Why should this have been the case? The reasons given relate not to attainment, but rather to reasons connected with the effective domain of learning. What does this say about learning and teaching in science?

The extract reveals only some of the qualitative evidence collected, but is it possible to extrapolate these findings to the primary classroom? Could it be that if we had all girl groups and all boy groups for science in large primary schools that there would be an increase in attainment for both groups? In smaller schools, could having single gender groupings within a heterogeneous class provide benefits for all?

Personal response

Think about your own personal experience of grouping in school science. What was your preference? Why did you prefer this grouping? Were there any disadvantages to this strategy?

Have you noticed differences in the way in which girls and boys approach and carry out practical work in science? Make a note of your thoughts.

Practical implications and activities

Reflect on the following questions:

1. What do you think about the questions raised by the above extract?
2. Should we consider single gender grouping for science? What evidence do you have for drawing this conclusion?
3. Observe boys and girls in mixed gender grouping for science. Record what you notice.
4. Are there any gender-specific behaviours evident? If so, what are they? Record your findings.
5. Talk to boys and girls about their preferences in relation to grouping in science. What is their preference and what are the reasons for their choice? Compare your findings with those in the extract.

Would it be possible for you to investigate the effects on children of different groupings in science?

My experience is that it is possible, but that it is crucial to narrow the focus of the study; to try not to be too ambitious and try as far as possible to focus on one variable at a time. Consider what sort of measuring tools would be appropriate, the practical implications of how the data would be collected and, importantly, how it would be analysed. Other factors might also be significant, for example, the size of groups might be significant for both single gender or mixed gender groups. Other factors might need to be considered, even if they could not be controlled. What else might affect the quality of the learning of the groups?

Plan to build a research element into your teaching.

Further reading

Smith, M, and Roden, J (1994) 'Encouraging a positive attitude towards physical science amongst girls', *Issues in Education: The Canterbury Papers*, 2 (1) Summer.

Sukhnandan, L (2000) 'Ability grouping: what is the evidence?', chapter 18, in Sears, J and Sorensen, P (2000) *Issues in science teaching*. London: Routledge Falmer.

How?

How can peer and parent tutoring of science help to assist learning in science?

Before you read the following extract, read:

- Watts, M (2001) 'The PLUS factors of family science'. *International Journal of Science Education,* 23 (1), 83–95.

Read the whole article then focus on the discussion about the differences between children's and adults' learning.

Extract – Topping, K J, Peter, C, Stephen, P, and Whele, M (2004) 'Cross-age peer tutoring of science in the primary school: influence on scientific language and thinking', *Educational Psychology,* **24 (1), pp59–60 and 60–61. London: Carfax (Taylor & Francis Ltd).**

Theoretical advantages of peer and parent tutoring in science

Despite the paucity of substantive empirical research, peer tutoring and parental involvement in science have a number of potential and theoretical advantages. Early years children involved in science investigations at home could relate scientific ideas and skills to their own real life situation in the company of mature and highly valued adults. Whether tutored by parents at home or peers in school, they would have the opportunity to explore their nascent understanding through discussion, enjoying immediate feedback and possibly improving their general language development as well as their scientific vocabulary (Gallos, 1995). They could have their own personal demonstrations if all else failed. Apart from the value of the extra practice, generalisation and transferability could be developed.

Even more importantly, this could serve to improve the child's motivation, confidence and self-image. Improved attitudes to science might have enduring effects later in the educational system and possibly even affect later higher education or career choices. This could prove particularly important for any groups more than usually at risk of especially poor self-image as scientists. Additionally, parents or peers who acted as science tutors might themselves reap cognitive attitudinal and self-confidence gains, as with other forms of 'learning by teaching' (Topping, 2000, 2001; Topping and Ehly, 1998).

Previous studies of paired science

Three studies of parent tutored paired science are reported in Topping (1998). In one, all 26 children in a class of six-year-olds participated in a seven-week project, and a feedback questionnaire was completed by every family. The parents were extremely positive about their children's reactions to the paired science activities; almost all reported seeing more interest in and enjoyment of science in their children. Almost as high a proportion of children were perceived to have shown cognitive gains in understanding and communicating scientific ideas and applying scientific methods. In two thirds of cases the children seemed more confident about scientific matters and were generalising their curiosity to a wider range of issues beyond those in the pack.

The second study was of a class of 28 children aged seven and eight, of whom 26 chose to participate. All these families returned a questionnaire. Again, parents were generally positive about the children's reactions to the paired scientific activities; two thirds or more reported seeing more interest in and enjoyment of science in their children, together with increased understanding and an increase in questioning about everyday phenomena. A majority of children were felt to have benefited under every possible evaluative heading, although little more than half had definitely improved in their ability to give better explanations – possibly because short-term changes in children of this age are not so striking as in younger children. A substantial majority of parents felt they had benefited themselves. Classroom observation indicated that the children were more interested and confident in science in class and were better at testing out ideas practically. There was evidence of generalisation into practical investigations in science class work.

In the third study, the methodology was extended to four-year-old children in a nursery school, and also yielded encouraging results. There were 29 parent participants of whom 27 returned the evaluation feedback questionnaire. Almost all parents reported increased enjoyment in science in their children, three quarters reported increased questioning about science, and well over half reported observable gains in competence and confidence in science. Parents were also very positive about the children's gains in understanding and enjoyment. Many parents expressed surprise at the capabilities of their child and were pleased at the increased questioning. Some parents reported an impact on reading, with children increasingly likely to seek out science books. The participating nursery children who had older siblings spontaneously called paired science 'homework' and thought it was very special. Children were seen to ask more intelligent questions in class, and certainly increased their use of embedded scientific language. The co-ordinating teacher concluded 'The science activities stimulated imagination and promoted a feeling of awe and wonder, while allowing children to begin to control their own environment'.

Analysis

This interesting study noted that the development of deeper understanding and transferable skills in science requires continuous interactive discussion and feedback, and extended practice in various contexts for generalisation. While it might be difficult for teachers to facilitate this in the normal course of the day, peer tutoring might succeed. They developed the 'paired science' programme where experimental tutees were a whole class to seven- and eight-year olds and the tutors eight- and nine-year-olds. Previous research had focused on parent tutoring. The two short extracts provide a summary of the theory that underpinned both research areas.

The arguments put forward for parental involvement are attractive. Such experiences could be set in everyday contexts. They have the added advantage of possibly informing parents, not only about their child's progress in science, but also of aspects of science thereby potentially, if only in a limited way, contributing to the scientific literacy of this important and influential section of the wider community. Furthermore, this links with the current move towards the school becoming more open and a social centre for the whole community.

Considering the practicalities involved in parent tutoring, a number of questions can be asked. Do parents have time to spend undertaking practical science tasks with their children? Would they want to? Would there be the materials at home for the investigations that might be necessary? Might a negative reaction to the involvement provide a negative response that might then be counter-productive? Are there any equal opportunity issues surrounding the notion of parent tutoring? Might this initiative disadvantage those children who do not have the benefit of a traditional home life with supportive parents or significant others?

Peer tutoring within the school might be much more of a realistic proposition. On the face of it, it sounds like a good idea that younger children should benefit from the knowledge and experience of older ones, but are there counter arguments here? Why should older children spend time working with younger ones? The benefits to the younger ones might be obvious, but what of the older ones, wouldn't their time be better spent on working on more demanding tasks set at their own level? It is well known that helping someone to understand something may well increase one's own knowledge and understanding. My own research suggests that this is certainly the case when pairing more experienced teachers of science with new entrants to the profession, and in the case of differential subject knowledge pairing, when final-year science specialist students with non-science specialist students (Roden, 1991, 2003).

Topping *et al.* worked with children on paired science activities for two 30-minute sessions per week covering various topics. Qualitative informal observations indicated that gains were made in terms of social interaction, conversational skills, questioning and experimentation. The extract talks of activities, but fails in this paper to explain the nature of the activities except in general terms. We might ask what activities would be appropriate in science? There needs to be a benefit for both tutor and learner. How can this be achieved?

Personal response

What is your response to the notion of peer and parent tutoring in science? Have you come across this idea before? Do you have any personal experience of it? How successful was it?
Make a note of your responses.

Practical implications and activities

Task 1
Work with a science co-ordinator or another science 'specialist'.

Consider either parent tutoring or peer tutoring.

1. What do you think are the advantages and disadvantages of your chosen grouping? Make a list.

2. Before the project was started, what steps would you take to make sure it was feasible?

Consider the practical aspects of parent or peer tutoring. If you chose peer tutoring, an example might be for Year 6 children to write a story for a younger audience as a starting point in science, e.g. about a kite and then make and test the kite with the younger child.

If you found the idea attractive, what sorts of activities do you think could be included in the scheme? Choose one of your ideas for further examination. Think through the practicalities of your idea, for example, in relation to parent tutoring:

- How would you introduce the idea?
- How would you present the material to make it accessible for a wide range of parental ability and interest?
- How could you solve the problem of resources?
- What methods could you use to monitor and evaluate the effectiveness of the initiative?

Task 2

Make a note of the kinds of activities provided for and engaged in Watts' (2001) article.

What sorts of activities were the family groups involved in? Could any of these ideas for science activities be applied in your classroom?

Write down some possibilities. Could these be applied to a small-scale situation with your class?

What were the difficulties encountered in the project reported by Watts?

In your prior reading, Watts (2001) explores the nature of children's learning and adult learning. What relevance does this have to a small-scale home/school initiative in science?

Make a note of your conclusions about incorporating such a project in your teaching.

Further reading

Topping, K J (1998) *The paired science handbook: parental involvement and peer tutoring in science.* London: Fulton; Bristol, PA: Taylor and Francis.

Topping, K J (2001) *Peer assisted learning: a practical guide for teachers.* Cambridge, MA: Brookline Books.

7 Formative assessment

By the end of this chapter you should have:

- considered **why** formative assessment is important in science;
- reflected on **what** the characteristics of formative assessment in science are;
- analysed **how** to use research into formative assessment to inform practice.

Linking your learning

Sharp, J, Peacock, G, Johnsey, R, Simon, S, and Smith, R (2002) *Achieving QTS. Primary science: teaching theory and practice.* Exeter: Learning Matters

Professional standards for QTS
1.7, 3.1.2, 3.1.3, 3.2.1, 3.2.2, 3.2.3, 3.2.4, 3.2.5

Introduction

You will be aware of the similarities and differences between formative and summative assessment. Black and Wiliam (2003, p623) tell us that these two terms apply not to the assessment, but to the functions they serve. Formative assessment informs learning and arises out of diagnostics testing in the 1970s, whereas summative assessment takes place at the end of episodes of teaching and is not usually useful for informing day-to-day planning for learning. In science, formative assessment has a long history. Unfortunately, unlike in mathematics where diagnostic assessment focused on children's misconceptions, science followed a Piagetian approach that sought to understand scientific reasoning in terms of stages of development and did not lead directly to application in normal teaching (Black and Wiliam, 2003).

The emphasis on Piagetian theory rather than constructivist theory was very familiar to those who were training to teach science in the primary school in the 1970s, as it underpinned both the Nuffield Primary Science and Schools Council Primary Science Projects. In my view, emphasis on ages and stages was to hinder significantly the development of science through the 1970s and 1980s, until the National Curriculum Task Group on Assessment and Testing (TEGAT) offered the view that teacher assessment lay at the heart of testing in the National Curriculum. Therefore they recommended that nationally prescribed tests would be marked by teachers, but be externally moderated (Black and Wiliam, 2003). Teachers received this notion with hostility on in-service sessions at the time. Later, this model was abandoned, but teacher assessment remained at the heart of science in the National Curriculum. Unlike English and mathematics, at the time of writing, there is no National Test at Key Stage 1, rather the weighting for teacher assessment is 50 per cent for Scientific Enquiry (Sc1) and 50 per cent for the three other Programmes of Study (PoS). At Key Stage 2 teacher assessment is supplemented by summative National Tests where the weighting of the elements of the PoS is 40 and 60 per cent respectively.

Black and Wiliam (2003) report the decline of formative assessment in the late 1980s. The move towards what we now term 'assessment for learning' began in 1997 leading to the influential publications 'Inside the Black Box' (Black and Wiliam, 1998). This led to the Kings-Medway-Oxfordshire Formative Assessment Group (KMOFAP) which aimed to help teachers put assessment for learning into practice in the classroom through supporting their own professional practice. In short, this was a research project where there was the clear intention to inform and influence practice. The project has made a particular impact on the understanding of formative assessment in science education; also, because of the fundamental link between assessment, evaluation and planning, the understanding of aspects of practice in science education have been elucidated. In the light of this, this chapter will examine the fundamental links between teaching, learning and assessment in science and provide an opportunity for reflection on your own practice.

Why?

Why is formative assessment important in science?

Which aspect of science do you find most difficult to assess?

Write a few sentences to say why you find this difficult.

Before you read the following extract, read:

- Sharp, J, Peacock, G, Johnsey, R, Simon, S and Smith, R (2002) 'Assessment, recording and reporting', chapter 8, in *Achieving QTS. Primary science: teaching theory and practice.* This chapter provides the background to formative assessment and examines the strategies that can be used by teachers.
- QCA (2003) 'Assessing progress in science', teacher's guide, QCA. **www.qca.org.uk/progress** in science. This consists of two packs of teaching/ assessment materials intended to be used, adapted and extended by teachers for use in the classroom at Key Stages 1 and 2. Familiarise yourself with the pack related to your key stage.

Extract: QCA (2003a) *Assessing progress in science teacher's guide*, **pp4–9. London: QCA (Enterprises) Ltd.**

Introduction
The message to teachers implicit in the 'Assessing Progress in Science' series is a simple one – you will be a more successful teacher by:

> making active enquiries into the sense your children are making of what you intend to teach, and modifying your teaching in the light of the children's understanding that you reveal.

This is the 'in a nutshell' message'. The process of gathering feedback about children's current ideas and acting upon it in order to enhance their understanding and further progress is referred to as 'formative assessment'. The purpose of formative assessment is to gather information while there is still time and opportunity to act upon its implications.

Assessment activities have an important function in gathering information from time to time, from place to place, so that teachers can check on children's progress … assessment activities enable teachers to sample progress in understanding of some key ideas. Teachers may choose to collect such information prior to the introduction of a new topic, during that topic or towards its completion. This can happen (indeed *should* happen) at any time during any key stage.

The purposes of assessment

Assessment is always carried out for a purpose, and there are a variety of purposes for which assessment is used. Assessment, which is valid and reliable, can be invaluable in offering rigorous, systematic information to teachers to inform action.

Formative assessment is used to collect information about performance before a task is complete. Such feedback offers the opportunity of modifying the conditions of learning even while it is still happening. It may be that formative assessment confirms that everything is proceeding according to plan. Alternatively, it may be that progress is not as expected. For example, the material a child is engaged with may fail to offer any challenge and a faster pace or more advanced material would be more appropriate. Formative assessment may be initiated by the teacher – 'How are you getting on?' – or by the child – 'How am I doing? Is this what you meant? Am I doing it right?' It may be that formative assessment reveals a problem – maybe one whose solution is not immediately apparent. When assessment is used to identify the nature of a problem in achieving expected or desirable outcomes, it is referred to as *diagnostic assessment*.

Teachers are encouraged to undertake formative assessment because the time and energy invested will result in more effective and satisfying teaching and learning outcomes for them and their children. Formative assessment has the potential to make teachers' jobs easier by enabling them to:

- inform their management of teaching and learning by offering insights into the learning needs of their children;
- help children to achieve the learning outcomes which are of immediate importance by focusing support exactly where it is needed;
- support children in the longer term in becoming more effective learners by helping them to develop techniques for self-monitoring and metacognitive learning.

The expression – 'teaching and learning' – is used (rather than each verb singly) to emphasise that classroom learning outcomes are the product of interactions between teachers and children, a series of iterations in which meanings and understandings are constantly subjected to explicit checks. Learning, redefined as 'sense making', has to involve the active participation of learners. Only relatively trivial outcomes are learned by receiving information that is memorised unchanged, and even this process requires a level of motivation.

The implication might well be that formative assessment causes curriculum coverage to take slightly longer than the direct 'top-down' route of transmission of facts. If this is the case, the justification is that the rate at which children achieve understanding is likely to be faster and the outcomes more likely to be integrated with their existing schemas. One consequence of a better integrated understanding is that children may be more able to use and apply what they have learned. Because the interactions are more effective, the learning outcomes are expected to be more efficient in the sense of achieving enduring understanding.

Assessing progress in science flowchart

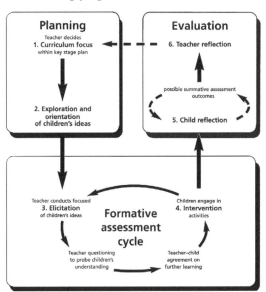

The planning activities are those that prepare the curriculum agenda and set the scene for children

1. *The curriculum focus indicates the learning agenda set by the teacher*. This focus will take into account the curriculum coverage responsibilities for the year group taught. While assessment for learning has some characteristics of what used to be known as a 'child-centred' approach, the teacher is clearly directing and guiding learning outcomes.

2. *Exploration and orientation* acknowledge that children are likely to require at least some degree of 'tuning into' the topic to be taught. This may include a review of previous teaching. Some direct experiences that reassure them that they have prior knowledge which allows them to make contact with the subject matter are also likely to be motivating.

The formative assessment cycle can take seconds, minutes, hours or even longer, depending on the particular context. The intervention is tailored to what emerges from the process of finding out existing ideas.

3. *Elicitation* is the process of requiring and enabling children to make explicit the ideas inside their heads. The exploration and orientation phase should ensure that children are clear about the context the teacher has set. Ideas should then be expressed when they have had time to reflect in a considered manner on what they believe.

4. *Intervention* is used as a term rather than an expression such as 'teaching' in order to reflect the fact that experiences that encourage children to reconsider and develop their ideas can take a variety of focused and strategic forms.

Reflective teachers and children will review what targets they set themselves and what has been achieved. Both may have summative feedback available on occasions, in the form of examination or other assessment results.

5. *Children's reflection* on their understanding, rather than unreflective rote learning is expected. The idea of metacognitive activity is that children are increasingly encouraged to think about what they know and how they know it. If any form of summative assessment is used, child reflection may include a constructively self-critical review of their performance.

6. *Teacher reflection* acknowledges that classroom strategies are adopted and developed when they prove to be positive and are adjusted when they reveal problems. Formative assessment is readily adopted as integral to reflective practice. Individual teachers' practices should also inform planning at the school level.

Analysis

Russell and McGuigan take as their starting point that assessment is fundamental to teaching and learning in science. They are advocating a system whereby, once outline planning of what should be taught has been completed, the chosen learning and recording activities simultaneously serve two functions, i.e. one related to learning and the other related to assessment. On the face of it, this strategy is attractive, but two questions can be asked: What does this approach imply for practice and how can this approach be put into operation?

Applying the principles of formative assessment in science requires teachers to start by clearly recognising and defining the learning outcome intention, followed by deciding what specifically is to be taught and deriving activities that will enable children to show their understanding. To achieve optimum efficiency children need to produce a 'product' that is matched exactly to the learning intention, thereby producing activities that will be easy to assess while at the same time providing 'evidence' for assessment purposes. This is not easy, but this is the key to formative assessment.

This approach is different to that used by many teachers. Teachers often start their planning by choosing the activity rather than matching the activity to a specific learning intention. The next step is often to differentiate a chosen activity for different groups in the class and then rigidly structure the next stage of planning around this. The formative assessment approach to teaching is different and requires more flexible planning.

You will be familiar with the term 'start where the children are' and may well have undertaken work aimed at a diagnostic approach to teaching. Experience tells us, however, that trainees' opportunity to engage in this approach is often directly related to the teaching and learning strategies employed within their particular placement. If this has been your experience, you should not reject the model without reflection. Basically, Russell and McGuigan's stance is that any teacher can adopt the essential strategies and that this process can be applied to both the assessment of scientific enquiry as well as scientific understanding. Their approach uses level descriptors as starting points, which, as you will see contradicts some of Harlen's views on formative assessment in the next extract.

Personal response

What is your response to this approach to formative assessment in science? Do you believe that you use assessment effectively for learning? To what extent is your planning flexible? Do you 'start where the children are'?

Practical implications and activities

Task 1

OFSTED (2005, p16, para 55) reports that *systems for assessment are often too heavily focused on what pupils have been taught, or on their attitudes and efforts, rather than assessing what they have learned.*

Reflect on this statement in relation to your own teaching.

- Describe how you plan for science to a colleague. Identify the *process* you go through in planning a lesson. Make a list of the stages you go through, e.g. do you start with the learning intention, or something else? What comes next? At what stage do you think about how you will assess your children? When do you decide on success criteria? Do you 'build in' assessment opportunities into your planning?
- Analyse your approach to planning. Are your plans flexible? Do you share your learning intentions with the children? Do you set targets in science? What sort of targets do you set?

Task 2

OFSTED (2005, p2), reports that day-to-day assessments to improve children's learning continues to be too weak and that too many children are given work that is not matched well enough to their needs.

Working with a colleague, examine your plans and analyse your children's work. Look at your records and the children's profiles.

1. Do your learning intentions provide you with a clear indication of what sort of evidence you need to collect about children's learning?
2. Do your lesson plans offer opportunities for children to demonstrate their understanding (including aspects of scientific enquiry)?
3. Do you try to match children's work within your plans?
4. Write down some of the targets you set for your children.
5. Analyse these – are they related both to scientific understanding and scientific enquiry?
6. What sort of evidence do you collect to support the conclusions you reach about children's learning in science. What guides your assessment?

Further reading

Naylor, S and Keogh, B (2004) *Thinking learning and assessment in science*, London: David Fulton/Sandbach: Millgate House Publishers. Here the authors provide many examples of active assessment in science and show how creative links can be made between thinking, learning and assessment.

What?

What are the characteristics of formative assessment in science?

Before you read the following extract, read:

- Ward, H (2005) 'Planning and assessing learning' chapter 6, pp80–98, in Ward, H, Roden, J, Hewlett, C and Foreman, J *Teaching science in the primary classroom*. London: PCP.
- Harlen, W (2000) 'Interpreting evidence for formative assessment', chapter 10, in *Teaching learning and assessing science 5-12* (3rd edn). London: PCP.

Extract: Harlen, W and Winter, J (2004) 'The development of assessment for learning: learning from the case of science and mathematics', *Language Testing*, **21 (3), 394–408. London: Hodder Arnold Journals.**

In science, the goals of learning are a combination of the development of conceptual understanding, skills of investigative enquiry and scientific attitudes. The process of learning is seen as the progressive development of understanding, in which new experience is linked to existing ideas. The 'linking' in science involves using existing ideas to try to make sense of new experience, a process that involves making a prediction based on existing ideas and seeing if the evidence of the new experience supports the prediction. This means gathering and interpreting relevant data; in short, using the skills of enquiry. In this process, ideas are extended to encompass more experience and the ideas become more widely applicable, more useful and more abstract. The relevant point in the present context is that the development of understanding depends on the use of the enquiry skills (and the attitudes that energise their use) and so these skills have to be developed and used scientifically. Consequently classroom assessment that helps learning in science must encompass concepts, skills and attitudes.

Using indicators of progress
Information about these learning goals can be gathered during teaching by several methods:

- observing learners when they are involved in practical (hands-on) investigation;
- questioning and discussing;
- studying the products of work, including drawings and concept maps as well as writing;
- listening and paying particular attention to the words learners use.

Often teachers use a combination of these methods in order to gain the fullest picture possible of a learner's progress, but in all cases it is important to have in mind what to look for or to listen for so that the information gained is relevant to the learning goals. Since the purpose of the assessment is to help development of ideas, skills and attitudes – and to use this information to identify next steps in pupil's learning – it is necessary to have the development mapped out, that is, to see the development towards the achievement of goals as a progression. Determining where the pupil is in this progression enables the teacher to identify the 'next step' towards the goals and thus the action needed to help this step to be taken. Although not enough is known to be definitive about the course of development of some of these learning outcomes, it is useful to use what we do know from research and experience to provide a focusing framework. For example, in science, in the development of conceptual understanding development can be described in terms of how pupils use the concept in giving an explanation or making a prediction. The following statements begin with ones indicating a limited understanding followed by progressively greater understanding indicated by wider application of the concept. Pupils:

- do no more than describe the situation rather than explaining it;
- use their own preconceived ideas rather than the relevant scientific ones;
- refer to relevant ideas without showing how they apply;
- apply the relevant ideas only in situations similar to those already encountered;
- apply the relevant ideas in situations different from those encountered before;
- bring several relevant ideas together to give a reasoned explanation or prediction.

These generic statements have to be 'translated' into the context of particular activities. So, for instance, if a teacher is looking at how well pupils understand adaptation of living things to their environment, and the activity is about camouflaged animals, the teacher would be paying attention to how the pupils explained observed differences between the colour of animals living in different habitats.

The products of work in defining the sequence of developments of ideas and skills have been variously described as 'progress maps' (Masters and Forster, 1996) and 'developmental indicators' (Harlen, 2000). Indeed, the sequence of levels of attainment in the National Curriculum and similar documents can be regarded as rather coarse-grained progress maps. These describe in very general terms what pupils do when operating at each of eight levels spanning the ages 5-16 ('observe, communicating findings in simple ways' at level 1 to 'decide which observations are relevant and include details in their records' at level 8).

For the purpose of using classroom assessment to help learning, however, there is no need to relate to stages of levels; what is important is to describe how a skill or understanding develops. While teachers and, increasingly learners, have become familiar with the language of levels, it is important to remember that these are a reporting tool, to convey information about progress at set times in a learner's school life, and do not have great value in supporting teachers in making day-to-day decisions about how to move learners on.

Lists of behaviours indicating progression in enquiry skills and scientific attitudes appropriate to learners aged 5–12 years have been developed by Harlen (2000, see p.149, for example). With the behaviours described in maps or lists such as these in mind, teachers are more able to gather evidence from observations and listening that is relevant to assessing progress. By comparing this evidence with the criteria they can gauge the point in development where learners are operating. The next step for the learners might be to consolidate skills at this point or to move towards the next point in the development.

Questioning and listening

Questioning is a major part of teachers' classroom interactions with learners and has a key role in classroom assessment. However, as Black *et al.* (2003) point out, many teachers do not plan what to say and what questions to ask so that they can help pupils to learn. There are two main aspects to questioning practice we consider here. One is the type of question asked and the other is the timing, particularly the time allowed for answering.

When the purpose of questioning is to find out learners' ideas and how they are linking new experience to their existing mental frameworks, the questions should invite more than a one-word answer; they should encourage learners to say what they really think, not to guess what answer the teacher is looking for. Changing a question from, for example, 'why do we eat food?' to 'why do you think we eat food?' makes a significant difference to the kind of answer learners feel is required. The latter gives an invitation to learners to express their own ideas, whilst the former suggests that a particular answer is expected. The same change can be made when the response is not a spoken answer to a question but a piece of written work or a drawing. For instance, if the teacher asks learners 'draw what you think is happening inside the incubating egg' the result is more likely to help the teacher to identify the ideas that the learners have than by asking for a drawing of the egg.

Analysis

Harlen has been involved in research and development of primary science over the last 40 years. In this extract with Winter, she clearly explains why you need to consider assessment for learning in terms of skills, concepts and attitudes. She encourages you to adopt a researcher's attitude to assessment – using the skills of enquiry. This is a good way to think about the whole process and can lead to an action research type approach to your teaching and assessment.

What Harlen and Winter call 'indicators of practice' provide pointers for planning, e.g. when will you observe your children? What will you be looking for? When will you listen to your children? What are you listening for, e.g. in terms of misconceptions or misunderstandings that might be revealed? Later the 'focusing frame' derived from research provides you with a simple checklist for analysis of children's understanding. This implies that you are familiar with the misconceptions that children might raise in the course of teaching. As you will appreciate, careful thought about teacher questions should be part of your planning, but what questions are most effective and for what purpose?

Interestingly, in this extract, (because all extracts need to be considered in the context in which they are written) Harlen and Winter maintain that level descriptors have little role in formative assessment and should be used summatively and for reporting purpose. I believe this view stems from Harlen's long-argued view that planning should be derived from the PoS and not from level descriptors. In practice, teachers did plan, usually exclusively, from the detailed level descriptors in the 1989 version of the science National Curriculum rather than from the PoS as was the intention. However, the question must be whether level descriptors *can* be used in formative assessment as Russell and McGuigan (2003) and Ward (2005) challenge.

Personal response

- Reflect on the extent to which you currently assess children's skills, knowledge and attitudes?
- What is your view of the use of level descriptors for assessment purposes?
- Can you identify any gaps in your assessment for learning?

Practical implications and activities

Task 1

Compare and contrast the two extracts above.

Task 2

Ward (2005, p. 80–98) puts forward strategies for implementing assessment for learning in science. Compare these strategies to those of your own.

Further reading

Harlen, W and Qualter, A (2004) 'Assessment' section 3, chapters 12 – 15, in *The teaching of science in primary schools*, (4th edn). London: David Fulton.

Harlen, W (1999) 'Purposes and procedures for assessing science process skills', *Assessment in Education*, 6, (1).

Markwick, A, Jackson, A and Hull, C (2003) 'Improving learning using formative marking and interview assessment techniques', *School Science Review*, 85 (311). Although this is written from a secondary perspective it provides insight into the practice and value of incorporating formative marking and interview as techniques for improving the effectiveness of teaching and learning.

How?

How can research into formative assessment inform practice?

Before you read the following extract, read:

- Harlen, W and Qualter, A (2004) 'Using information for formative assessment: deciding and communicating next steps', chapter 16, in *The teaching of science in primary schools*. (4th edn.) London: David Fulton.

Extract: Torrance, H and Pryor, J (2001) 'Developing formative assessment in the classroom: using action research to explore and modify theory'. *British Educational Research Journal*, 27 (5). London: Carfax (Taylor & Francis Ltd).

TASK identified two 'ideal – typical' approaches to formative assessment, which nevertheless were not necessarily mutually exclusive in practice: one 'convergent', the other 'divergent' (see Table 1). These ideal types seemed to be associated with teachers' differing views of learning and of the relationship of assessment to the process of intervening to support learning, and might be said to represent a continuum of possibilities for classroom teachers. In convergent assessment, the important thing is to find out if the learner knows, understands, or can do a predetermined thing. It is characterised by detailed planning, and is generally accomplished by closed or pseudo-open questioning and tasks. Here the interaction of the learner with the curriculum is seen from the point of view of the curriculum. The theoretical origins of such an approach would appear at least implicitly to be behaviourist, deriving from mastery-learning models and involving assessment of the learner by the teacher. Divergent assessment, on the other hand, emphasises the learners' understanding rather than the agenda of the assessor. Here, the important thing is to discover what the learner knows, understands and can do. It is characterised by less detailed planning, where open questioning and tasks are of more relevance. The implications of divergent teacher assessment are that a constructivist view of learning is adopted, with an intention to teach in the zone of proximal development (Vygotsky, 1986). As a result, assessment is seen as accomplished jointly by the teacher and the student, and orientated more to future development rather than measurement of past or current achievement.

CONVERGENT ASSESSMENT	DIVERGENT ASSESSMENT
Assessment which aims to discover *if* the learner knows, understands or can do a predetermined thing. This is characterised by:	Assessment which aims to discover *what* the learner knows, understands or can do. This is characterised by:
Practical implications a. precise planning and an intention to stick to it;	**Practical implications** a. flexible planning or complex planning which incorporates alternatives;
b. tick-lists and can-do statements;	b. open forms of recording (narrative, quotations etc.);
c. an analysis of the interaction of the learner and the curriculum from the point of view of the curriculum;	c. an analysis of the interaction of the learner and the curriculum from the point of view of the learner and the curriculum;
d. closed or pseudo-open questions and tasks;	d. open questioning and tasks;
e. a focus on contrasting errors with correct responses;	e. a focus on miscues – aspects of learners' work which yield insights into their current understanding, and on prompting metacognition;
f. judgemental or quantitative evaluation;	f. descriptive rather than purely judgemental evaluation;
g. involvement of the student as recipient of assessments.	g. involvement of the student as initiator of assessments as well as recipient.
Theoretical implications h. a behaviourist view of learning;	**Theoretical implications** h. a social constructivist view of learning;
i. an intention to teach or assess the next predetermined thing in a linear progression;	i. an intention to teach in the zone of proximal development;
j. a view of assessment as accomplished by the teacher.	j. A view of assessment as accomplished jointly by the teacher and the student.
This view of assessment might be seen less as formative assessment, rather as repeated summative assessment or continuous assessment.	This view of assessment could be said to attend more closely to contemporary theories of learning and accept the complexity of formative assessment.

Table 1. Convergent and divergent classroom assessment

Analysis

How can research inform formative assessment practice? Harlen advises the use of an investigative approach to assessment for learning in science, therefore you should see yourself as a researcher in this respect. The last extract in this chapter takes the notion of teacher-as-researcher as its starting point and it may well provide messages of value for your practice. Adopting an 'action research' approach, Torrance and Pryor (2001) focused on primary practice, but not on science in particular. Nevertheless, their contribution is relevant here not least because they first identified and then compared two distinct approaches to formative assessment in practice. The first question to ask is whether these models reflect your experience and practice of formative assessment.

It is possible to challenge some points in the extract. Categorising aspects of practice can sometimes lead to the adoption of rigid views. For example, one of the characteristics of divergent assessment is the use of tick sheets and 'can do' statements, but do these necessarily result in what the writers term repeated summative assessment or continuous assessment? Could it have a use in formative assessment? If so, what might that purpose be?

Supporting aspects of the previous extracts, flexible planning is identified as important in formative assessment. Why is flexible planning so important and does this reflect current practice?

There is no specific mention of targets in the extract, but it is appropriate to consider OFSTED's view here. OFSTED (2005, p17) advocate that teachers provide the opportunity for children to evaluate their own work to identify areas for improvement, but point out that within inspections it is evident that children are often unclear how to go about meeting the targets set. Although more schools now try to ensure that children are aware of their targets, not all children are involved in setting them and children are not clear about what targets mean or what they need to do to improve.

Personal response

Can you identify with the statements above and identify which model reflects your current practice?

Practical implications and activities

Task 1
- Copy the chart in the extract and use a highlighter pen to record your position in relation to each statement in the grid.
- Are you convergent or divergent in your assessment of children in science?
- Record your conclusions.

Task 2
Video yourself teaching science. With a colleague, analyse your teaching in relation to aspects of the categories above. In particular focus on and analyse your questioning and your response to children during the lesson.

Observe your plenaries. For what purpose do you use these?

OFSTED's (2005, p 16) view is that *the most effective teachers use the plenary flexibly sometimes with mini-plenaries undertaken at key points either during the week or in lessons.* Is this a common feature of your own teaching? What conclusions do you come to about your own practice? Could you improve your assessment of learning in your classroom?

Task 3

Do you use tick lists and 'can do' statements in your teaching, and if so, how?

Look again at Ward's (2005, p85-88) advice about the use of level descriptors in planning. Could you use the level descriptors to write 'can do' statements as targets for short-term learning?

Task 4

Revisit the grid you highlighted earlier. Now review your ideas about what your practice should be like and, with a colleague or mentor, set yourself targets for future development.

Further reading

Harlen, W and Qualter, A (2004) 'Involving children in assessing their work', chapter 17 in *The teaching of science in primary schools*, (4th edn). London: David Fulton.

Black, P and Wiliam D (2003) 'In praise of educational research: formative assessment', *British Educational Research Journal*, 29 (5).

8 Summative assessment

By the end of this chapter you should have:

- considered **why** teachers may need to review their practice of preparing children for the National Tests in science;
- reflected on **what** demands the National Tests make on children at Key Stages 1 and 2 and how this impacts on teaching science in the primary sector;
- analysed **how** children's achievement in National Tests can be promoted.

Linking your learning

Sharp, J, Peacock, G, Johnsey, R, Simon, S, and Smith, R, chapter 8 (2002) *Achieving QTS. Primary science: teaching theory and practice*. Exeter: Learning Matters.

Professional Standards for QTS
1.7, 3.2.1–3.2.5

Introduction

Russell (1998) charts the development of the Key Stage 2 standards tests and provides some useful insights into national performance of Year 6 pupils, the performance of subgroups within the Year 6 cohort, and the level of individual understanding. There was a strongly held perception among teachers that the National Tests in science largely tested the ability to recall facts. Russell (1998, p134) reminds us that:

> It was the firm requirement that from the outset that Experimental and Investigative science should not be assessed by the standard tests, but would be left to teacher assessment. Teachers regarded this as the imposition of an unmanageable curriculum and assessment regime, non-inclusion of Sc1 in the tests provoked particular criticism.

This short extract provides a telling insight into the reaction not only of teachers to the science tests but also of those who were trying to promote primary science education from outside school. Under the Curriculum 2000, 'Experimental and Investigative Science' became essentially what is now Scientific Enquiry. The non-inclusion of some items had a number of unintended outcomes. First, that early tests appeared to many to only address a narrow range of scientific knowledge which led directly to 'teaching to the test', and second, that although there was a great emphasis on the skills of scientific enquiry in the National Curriculum Programmes of Study (PoS), teachers tended to ignore this aspect of science. This apparent lack of status of Sc1 was reflected in practice in many primary classrooms. Despite successive QCA reports (c.f. QCA 1998, 1999, 2000, 2001) into the analysis of performance recommending that children's performance would be enhanced by the inclusion of more practical 'hands on' work in science, this advice was largely ignored.

Change in the science National Curriculum test items was introduced in 2003. This led Stringer (2003) to ask, 'Is this a fair test?'. He predicted that the longer, more enquiry-focused test would result in lower scores for many primary schools as the questions moved from recall of facts to testing children's wider science skills. Essentially, he said, the questions would emphasise thinking and observational skills:

> Children will be asked what an activity is designed to find out, and how it might be done. They will need to identify which factors they are changing and what they are observing and measuring – and what factors they need to control to ensure any test is being conducted fairly. They will also be asked if it is possible to pre-dict outcomes and they will need to know how to present and interpret results and whether the results will match their predictions. They will need to evaluate how good the evidence is, how it might be improved, and whether it supports any prediction (Stringer, 2003 **www.tes.co.uk/search/story/?story.id=375827**)

The changes in the test challenged teachers' perceptions of the test and should have led to a corresponding change of practice. However, change in practice is often resisted even in the face of challenges such as these. Teachers' ideas about teaching science are often as difficult to change as many children's ideas in science. The result was that although there was an increasing emphasis in the test items on higher-level aspects of science, reflecting the intention of the National Curriculum, the emphasis on rote learning and teaching to the test in the classroom, particularly in Year 6, continued.

It is with these issues in mind that this chapter aims to give you an insight into the demands of the End of Key Stage National Tests for science and how children can be prepared to maximise achievement.

Why ?

Why should teachers review their practice of preparing children for the National Tests in science?

Before you read the following extract:

- familiarise yourself with Year 6 teaching in your school or a school that is known to you;
- find out how the school prepares the children for National Tests at the end of Year 6.

Make a note of your findings.

Extract: QCA (2005a) *National Curriculum Tests 2004: implications for teaching and learning from the 2004 tests.* **London: QCA (Enterprises) Ltd.**

Key Stage 2 science
These implications are derived from an analysis of how pupils performed in the 2004 tests.

Well done: some examples of progress and continued success

Almost all pupils are able to:

- identify a safety precaution used in a photograph of burning materials;
- use the results from a simple experiment to predict what will happen in a similar situation;
- order the stages of growth in the human life cycle;
- recognise that temperature is a measure of how hot something is;
- identify the shadow of an object.

Most pupils are able to:

- use a table of results to find out specific data and identify simple patterns;
- name the stem as the part of the plant through which water travels to reach the flower;
- identify similar features of animals using observational skills;
- recognise where evaporation occurs in the water cycle;
- identify familiar materials that burn and do not burn, eg paper, fabric, metal, stone;
- use and construct classification keys.

Sc1 Scientific enquiry

To help improve performance, pupils need opportunities to:

- plan investigations, identifying the factors/variables involved and defining them specifically, e.g. volume of water rather than water; [A8, A3d, B5b,c]
- discuss why factors/variables may be irrelevant for a fair test; [A5d]
- think about what may happen in order to decide on the measurements to take, the most appropriate equipment to use and any safety risks involved; [A5a-c, A8b]
- use a variety of tables and graphs to read off data and identify trends and patterns in the data, looking out for unlikely results which may be inaccurate; [A7c-e, B5d]
- identify evidence in a table that allows a conclusion to be reached and discuss whether the evidence supports a prediction; [A3b, B5e]
- use comparative statements rather than absolute statements when comparing, eg 'the bulbs will be brighter' rather than 'the bulbs will be bright'. [B7c, B8b]

Sc2 Life processes and living things

To help improve performance, pupils need opportunities to:

- learn the life processes of plants and animals and relate them to particular parts of animals and plants; [A7b, B3c]
- relate 'life processes' to the mnemonic MRS NERG/GREN, if used; [B3b]
- learn the functions of the reproductive parts of the flower and the role of these in the life cycle of the plant; [B3d]
- discuss balanced diets and why they are important for good health; [A1a,b]
- use outdoor surroundings and information in books to construct different food chains and use correct terminology to describe the feeding relationships between the animals and plants in a food chain, paying attention to the arrow direction. [B4a,b]

Sc3 Materials and their properties

To help improve performance, pupils need opportunities to:

- experience a range of scientific changes, (eg dissolving, evaporation) that occur in different contexts and use the correct terminology to describe them; [A6a,b, B9c]

- explain why changes take place, eg liquids may turn solid when cooled; [A6e]
- hold different materials safely over a candle flame to see which materials burn, using the results to group the materials accordingly; [B1d]
- investigate a range of non-reversible changes including burning and recognise that all result in new material(s) being formed; [B1a,c, B6a]
- learn the different processes occurring at different stages in the water cycle and particularly where condensation occurs; [B9b]
- separate salt from water and discuss the similarities between this and evaporation from the ocean in the water cycle. [B9c]

Sc4 Physical processes

To help improve performance, pupils need opportunities to:

- show that sound is produced by vibrations and find out what happens to the sound as the distance from the sound source changes; [A2a,2b]
- recognise that sounds travels through materials other than air; [A2c]
- explain why some materials appear shiny; [B2a]
- explain how shadows form and identify which materials cause them to form; [B2c]
- find out how light travels so that we can see objects. Draw arrows, using a ruler, on a variety of diagrams to show light paths; [B2b]
- investigate with circuits the effects of adding different numbers of components or different numbers of cells and make comparisons; [B7aii,c,d]
- observe that friction is a force that acts in the opposite direction to movement and that it can be represented by an arrow. [A9ci]

Analysis

Every year the Qualifications and Assessment Authority analyse pupil performance on the National Tests and publish their findings as implications for teaching and learning. Findings in 2004 highlighted some strengths and weaknesses in relation to test questions. The conclusion was that teachers are providing opportunities for children to recognise safety measures and are able to predict. It also shows that children understand stages of growth in the human life cycle and can recognise temperature and the correct shadow of an object.

It is noticeable that almost every question in the 2004 tests is set in a practical context. This is consistent with the intention of the National Curriculum statutory orders where the development of knowledge and understanding of science should run alongside scientific enquiry. In other words, there is a statutory requirement for teachers to provide children with opportunities to undertake practical work alongside other aspects of learning in science. However, as we know, this is often not evident in practice, but the test items themselves clearly provide teachers with specific clues to the sorts of investigations and other practical activities that they should be providing for their children across the PoS. Teachers might well be advised to take notice of such information and revise schemes of work in the light of these. Successive school inspection reports for primary science, for example, Her Majesty's Inspectorate (HMI) (OFSTED/HMI, 2004), found that there had been a reduction in the time given to science and, particularly for investigative work. OFSTED reports frequently noted the lack of or poor quality of science in many primary schools. Couple this with anecdotal evidence of teachers teaching to the test and something seems not to add up. Looking at the bullet points for action in relation to the 2004 tests, one fails to see what more explicit guidance could be presented to teachers to guide planning for future practice. What is really going on in relation to practical work in the classroom? How can children score so highly on the tests (significantly 87 per cent achieving level 4 or 5) whilst at the same time OFSTED report lack of appropriate practical work in school?

All this raises a number of questions:

- Does it mean that practical work isn't required or do the tests examine short-term ability to respond to test items? If so, what is the role of practical work?
- What do children think about science in Year 6?
- What could be the long-term consequences of present practice in terms of children's attitudes and motivation towards science?
- What do teachers think about the way they teach science in Year 6?
- Does their practice reflect their views?
- What beliefs influence their practice in preparing children for the National Tests in science?

Questions like these should form the basis of your reflection.

Personal response

What is your response to the above extract and the analysis provided?

Practical implications and activities

How could the recommendations in the extract inform planning for teaching and learning?

Look at the following table:

Science National Test Results Key Stage 2, 2000 – 2004
(Percentage of cohort at each level)

Levels	Below 3	3	4	5
2000	3	11	50	34
2001	2	9	53	34
2002	2	9	49	38
2003	2	10	46	41
2004	1	10	43	43

Note: Rows do not total 100% as children who were absent or disapplied were not shown above

Source: QCA (2004)

What does the above table tell us about the trends in performance between 2000 and 2004?

- QCA (2004) report that historically, boys and girls perform better in different areas of the test as shown:

    - Boys: physical and technology topics, and more mathematical questions.

    - Girls: living things and the understanding or interpretation of written information.

In 2004 the tests overall show little difference in performance with respect to gender. They said:

- less than 10 per cent of individual 1-mark questions showed any difference in performance with respect to gender;

- these questions do not follow the patterns in learning as shown historically.

Why do you think this change might have occurred? Discuss this with an experienced science co-ordinator, or deputy headteacher.

Look at examples of test questions and compare the way they are presented. Is there a difference?

Further reading

Pollard, A, and Triggs, P (2000) *What pupils say: changing policy practice and experience.* London: Continuum.

What?

What demands do the National Tests make on children at Key Stage 2 and what does this imply for teaching science in the primary sector?

Before you read this extract:

- familiarise yourself with the Key Stage 2 National Tests in science and their assessment arrangements.

QCA (2004) 'The water cycle, Question 9'. *Key Stage 2 Science Test Paper B, levels 3–5.*
London: QCA (Enterprises) Ltd.

9   **The water cycle**

(a)   This picture shows part of the water cycle.

Tick **ONE** box to say what the arrow shows.

cold water rising ☐   water vapour condensing ☐

water evaporating ☐   gas changing to liquid ☐

9a
1 mark

(b)   Tick **ONE** box in each row to show if each sentence is **true**
or **false**.

Clouds form …

	True	False
from water produced by condensation.	☐	☐
from water vapour in the air.	☐	☐

9b
1 mark

(c)   In the water cycle, water from the sea becomes rain water.

Why is rain water **not** salty when it comes from salty sea water?

....

....

9c
1 mark

Total   20

Extract: QCA (2005b) 'Washing day, Question 2'. *Key Stage 2 Science Test Paper A, levels 3–5.* **London: QCA (Enterprises) Ltd.**

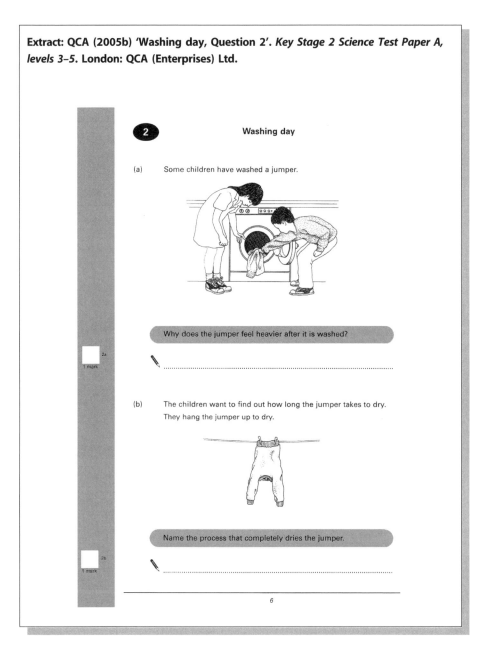

2   **Washing day**

(a)   Some children have washed a jumper.

Why does the jumper feel heavier after it is washed?

✎ ....

2a
1 mark

(b)   The children want to find out how long the jumper takes to dry.
They hang the jumper up to dry.

Name the process that completely dries the jumper.

✎ ....

2b
1 mark

6

(c)   The children weigh the jumper every hour.
        They make a graph of their results.

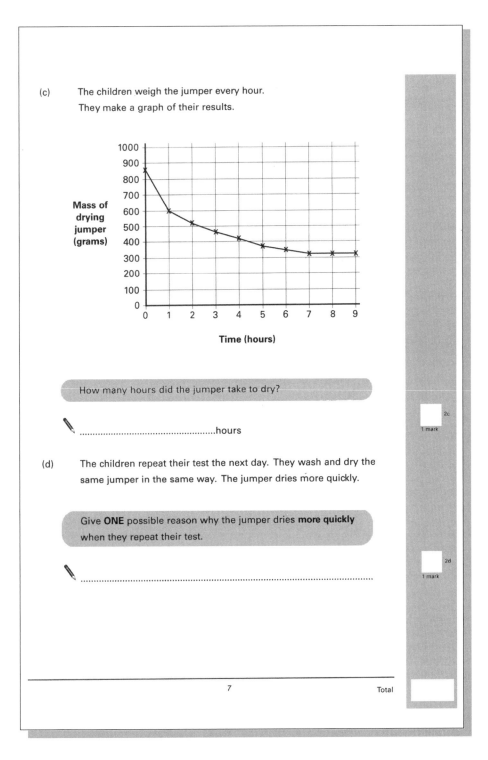

Time (hours)

How many hours did the jumper take to dry?

✎ ....hours

2c

1 mark

(d)   The children repeat their test the next day. They wash and dry the
        same jumper in the same way. The jumper dries more quickly.

Give **ONE** possible reason why the jumper dries **more quickly**
when they repeat their test.

✎ ....

2d

1 mark

Total

QCA (2002) 'Bathtime, Question 5'. *Key Stage 2 Science Test Paper A, levels 3–5.* London: QCA (Enterprises) Ltd.

3 **Bathtime**

(a) Jack gets out of the bath. He dries himself with a towel.

Why is towelling a good material to dry himself with?

✎ ....

3a
1 mark

(b) Small puddles of water drip on to the floor tiles and stay there.

Tick **ONE** box to say why the puddles stay on the floor tiles.

✎ The puddles stay on the floor because the floor tiles...

soak up water. ☐   bend easily. ☐

are waterproof. ☐   are solid. ☐

3b
1 mark

(c)   The bathroom window is closed.

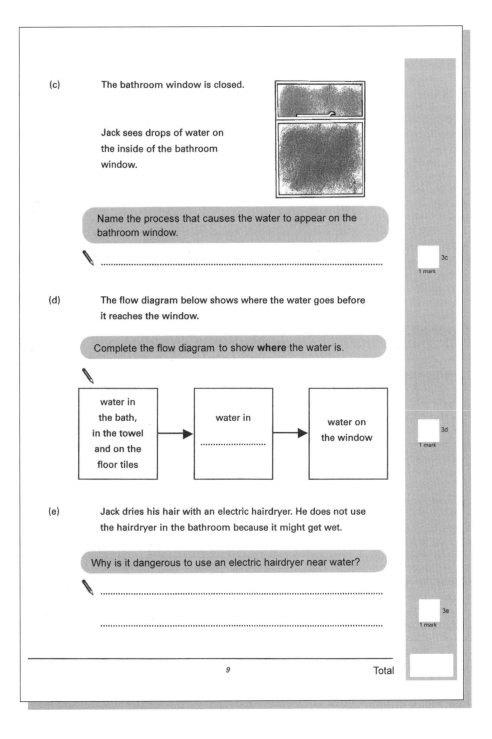

Jack sees drops of water on the inside of the bathroom window.

Name the process that causes the water to appear on the bathroom window.

....

3c

1 mark

(d)   The flow diagram below shows where the water goes before it reaches the window.

Complete the flow diagram to show **where** the water is.

| water in the bath, in the towel and on the floor tiles | water in .... | water on the window |

3d

1 mark

(e)   Jack dries his hair with an electric hairdryer. He does not use the hairdryer in the bathroom because it might get wet.

Why is it dangerous to use an electric hairdryer near water?

....

....

3e

1 mark

9   Total

QCA (2001) 'Drying sponge, Question 5'. *Key Stage 2 Science Test Paper B, levels 3–5.*
London: QCA (Enterprises) Ltd.

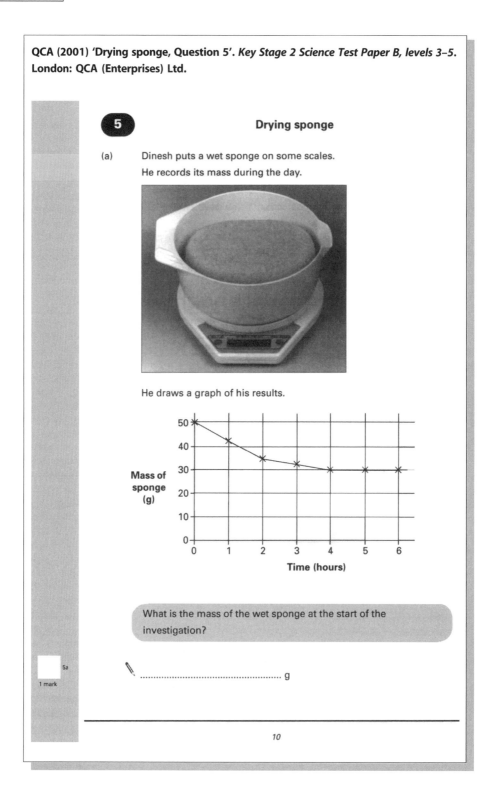

5   **Drying sponge**

(a)   Dinesh puts a wet sponge on some scales.

He records its mass during the day.

He draws a graph of his results.

Mass of sponge (g)

Time (hours)

What is the mass of the wet sponge at the start of the investigation?

5a

1 mark

.... g

10

(b) Describe how the mass of the wet sponge changes over the first four hours.

✎ ....

5b

1 mark

(c) What process causes the mass of the drying sponge to change?

✎ ....

5c

1 mark

(d) What is the mass of the dry sponge?

✎ .... g

5d

1 mark

(e) Some other children discuss Dinesh's results.
Look at their ideas below.

Use the graph to help you write **true** or **false** next to each idea.

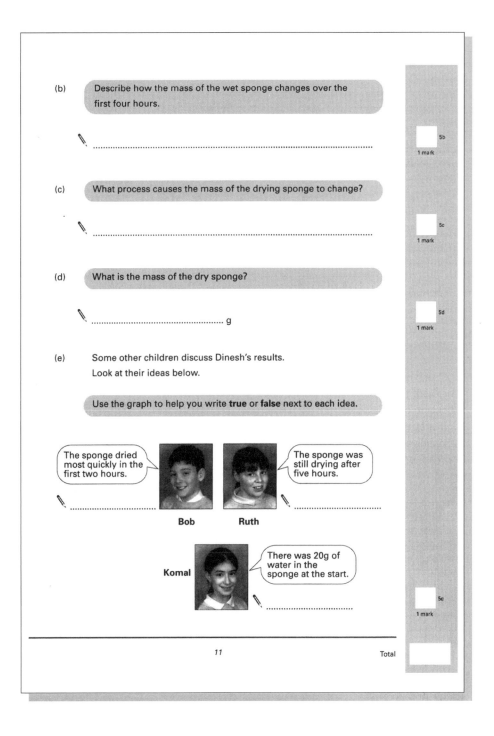

The sponge dried most quickly in the first two hours.

✎ ....

Bob

Ruth

The sponge was still drying after five hours.

✎ ....

Komal

There was 20g of water in the sponge at the start.

✎ ....

5e

1 mark

Total

QCA (2003b) 'Evaporation, Question 5'. *Key Stage 2 Science Test Paper B, levels 3–5.* **London: QCA (Enterprises) Ltd.**

5   Evaporation

(a)   Rose knows that water and vinegar evaporate.

Tick **ONE** box to show what **evaporation** means.

Evaporation is the change from...

gas to liquid. ☐   gas to solid. ☐

liquid to solid. ☐   liquid to gas. ☐

5a
1 mark

(b)   Rose sets up a test to find out if more water or more vinegar evaporates over 3 days.

She puts water in one container and vinegar in another container, like this:

Water   **Vinegar**

Rose places both containers on the same window sill.

(i)   Use the information above to describe **ONE** thing that is not fair in her test.

5bi
1 mark

....

(ii)   Why does it matter if her test is not fair?

....

5bii
1 mark

....

12

(c)   Rose changes her test to make it fair. She measures the volumes of water and vinegar twice each day to see how much has evaporated.

The table below shows her results.

Day	Time	Volume of water (cm³)	Volume of vinegar (cm³)
Monday	10am	100	100
	3pm	99	98
Tuesday	10am	97	94
	3pm	94	86
Wednesday	10am	91	82
	3pm	89	80

Rose wanted to compare water and vinegar to find out which evaporated the most over 3 days.

> Use Rose's results to write a conclusion for her test.

✎ ....

....

5c

1 mark

(d)   Rose notices that more water and vinegar evaporated between 10am and 3pm on Tuesday than between the same times on Monday or Wednesday.

> Suggest **ONE** possible reason why more water and vinegar evaporated on Tuesday.

✎ ....

5d

1 mark

III

Analysis

The five extracts have been selected because they cover similar areas of content drawn from Science 3 Materials and their properties PoS, that is, involving the change of state of water. What is noticeable is that although they appear to be testing related areas of knowledge, they are set in different contexts. What is the motive for this? Should teachers have included all these different scenarios within their scheme of work, or is there some other reason? Children are being asked about their *understanding* of the ideas and are asked to apply their understanding of the concept in a different context, thereby asking for application of knowledge rather than merely the recall of terms that was evident in earlier versions of the tests in science. We can also look for any difference in the style of the tests since 2001. Interestingly, looking again at the 2001 question, children were even then being asked to interpret data. Whilst this question might not be typical of others in that year, the type of question challenges the notion that tests before 2003 were mainly based on recall of facts. In fact, the 2002 question suggests even the 'why' question appears to be based on recall. Nevertheless, there is a distinct difference between the 2001 question and the question posed in 2005. Children were tested on whether they could recognise the process of evaporation, asked to interpret data, and then asked to provide a reason, in other words to explain why they think the event occurred. The question set in 2004 shows a fairly typical diagram of the water cycle. An objective look at the diagram reveals the potential for misconceptions, i.e. that evaporation only takes place over the sea and rain only falls on the land. The question is also heavily dependent on language ability, but what is it testing? Once again, it is some application of facts, i.e. but also a requirement for an explanation.

Analysis of questions like this can challenge teachers' perception of the nature of the tests and the demands placed on children. It suggests the kinds of activities that children can undertake throughout the key stage to give the experiences on which to base their understanding. Children need to know some basic facts of science to understand the concepts and apply these in a variety of contexts. Furthermore they need to be able to analyse data and draw conclusions from this. Although some might argue that children can learn this from practising test items that focus on the same context, this can never replace the learning that can be gained by children carrying out their own investigation, collecting their own data to form conclusions and then, finally to try to explain findings. This, rather than recall of facts, is what the National Test is testing and this is what QCA are recommending to improve pupil performance.

Personal response

What is your view of the test items above? What are the test items testing?
What are the implications of this for teaching and learning in the classroom?

Practical implications and activities

With a colleague:

- Look carefully at all the test items in Test A and Test B in 2005. What is each item demanding of the child?

- Look back at the short quotation from Stringer in the introduction to this chapter.
- Make a note of the sorts of items that are found in the tests. Write a list of the different challenges the 2005 test questions provide for children.
- Now use your list to find out how often children are asked to recall a fact. How often are they asked to explain? How often are they asked to read a measuring scale, e.g. a newtonmetre, etc.?
- What conclusions do you come to about the demands of the 2005 tests?
- What implications do you think your findings have for your own teaching and for schools' schemes of work?

How?

How can research findings inform practice in this area?

Before you read the following extract, read:

- Harlen, W and Deakin Crick, R (2003) 'Testing and motivation for learning', *Assessment in Education*, 10(2), 169–206.

Extract: Sturman, L (2003) 'Teaching to the test: science or intuition', *Educational Research*, 45(3 Winter) pp261–273. London: Taylor & Francis Ltd.

Koretz, McCaffrey and Hamilton (2001) note that the term 'test preparation' in common usage has a negative connotation. However, they distinguish seven types of test preparation. Three of which, they argue, can produce unambiguous, meaningful gains in test score. These are 'teaching more', 'working harder' and 'working more effectively'. In contrast, three strategies ('reallocation' of resources, 'alignment' of tests with curricula and 'coaching' of substantive elements) can lead to either meaningful or inflated gains, while the seventh strategy ('cheating') can lead only to inflated grades. Various preparation strategies have been reported for the science tests, representing several of these types of test preparation. These strategies include regular testing (Ellis, 1995) and the use of games (Patterson, 1999). Jurd (2000) reported 'booster groups' for borderline L4 pupils, and learning vocabulary lists as homework. Up to 20 per cent of teachers found evaluation reports of the previous years' tests (e.g. QCA, 2001a) useful in informing test preparation (Emery *et al.* 1998). Anecdotally, teachers also report using past test papers as practice tests, and 'question spotting' during testing week, whereby, topics not included in Test A are revised in case they appear in Test B.

In their study of tests across the Key Stage 2 core subjects, Brown *et al.* (1996) found that approximately half of the teachers involved considered that their preparation had increased children's test scores. However, no evidence was given to support such claims and, presumably, the other half of teachers felt that their preparation either had no impact or was detrimental.

[Other] studies suggest that we cannot take it for granted that preparation for National Tests will always lead to significant score increases. Preparation seems to arise from an intuitive belief that it can make a difference, rather than from evidence that it actually does. Despite this, research evidence shows that integrating assessment and learning can result in gains in both (Black and Wiliam, 1998), although these gains depend on the type and quality of feedback given, as well as on opportunities to work on areas needing improvement. Black and Wiliam argue that some apparent gains in test scores can be attributed to teachers (consciously or unconsciously) 'teaching to the test'. Nevertheless, their findings imply that test preparation aimed at consolidating understanding and based on key features of effective formative assessment might result in valid gains in test scores.

Analysis of frequencies: context, timing and focus

As expected, preparation for the science test was widespread, with 61 of the 64 teachers (95 per cent) preparing their pupils. The three teachers who did not prepare all worked in schools with fewer than ten Year 6 pupils, although three other teachers in such small schools did prepare their pupils. A few teachers noted that they engaged reluctantly in test preparation. One commented, for example:

> we are dismayed by the amount of time we have to spend in Year 6 on preparation for SATs

Such comments imply an element of compulsion. Interestingly, Gallagher and Smith (2000) reported that whilst teachers and parents believed that a school's test results affected its reputation, analysis showed no direct link between test performance and subsequent enrolment.

Of the teachers who prepared their classes, 32 reported that preparation activities replaced some of their normal science activities, whilst only six said that preparation replaced all other science activities. The small size of this latter figure is encouraging. Nevertheless, these data lend weight to Jurd's (2000) finding that some children experience a narrowing in their science education in Year 6, and this is reinforced by the following quote from one respondent: 'Preparation does mean that most experimental and investigative work is left until after SATs.'

In contrast, 22 teachers stated that their preparation was additional to other science activities. This raises the question: how did these teachers find time to prepare in this way, when others report that the required curriculum coverage makes it difficult to both teach and revise thoroughly? Insights can be gained from the following comments:

> I spent more time than I should doing science in the run up to SATs and am now redressing the balance.

> Revision was not purely for the test, but to revise knowledge gained as we do in all areas.

> As each block of work for Year 6 is taught, SATs questions relating to this area are covered/discussed, and children look at how questions are set.
>
> These quotes reveal two key strategies for fitting test preparation into the curriculum. One strategy involves reorganising the curriculum, so that tested areas are taught more thoroughly first; the other involves integrating test preparation directly into teaching. The first strategy has the potential disadvantage that the curriculum becomes segmented: some curriculum areas may receive limited attention with a consequent risk of reduced status. The second strategy might be subject to the same criticism, depending on how it is implemented, but has the advantage that the tests are seen as integral to learning and perhaps, therefore, less stressful for all concerned.
>
> Teachers varied in the timing of their test preparation with the school year beginning in September and the tests taking place in May, a Year 6 teacher could spend as little as a few days or weeks on preparation or as much as eight months … All 61 respondents who prepared did so with all pupils in their classes; none prepared only selected pupils. Just under one-third, however, gave *additional* support to particular groups. Perhaps not surprisingly, the most common focus of additional preparation was the borderline L4 group of pupils: 14 respondents (74 per cent of those who used additional preparation) targeted this group of pupils. Nevertheless, such targeting was less prevalent than might have been expected, involving less than a quarter of the total 61 respondents who prepared. Nine teachers targeted their borderline L5 pupils, a large proportion relative to those who targeted the more 'sensitive' L4 borderline.

Analysis

In the extract Sturman examines the teacher's practice in preparing children for National Tests in science and some issues involved in test preparation. In another article, Harlen and Deakin Crick (2003) look at findings of a systematic review of the impact of testing on children's motivation for learning. Together, these articles give insights into this problematic area. Naturally, teachers want to improve child performance and to raise the standards of the school, but this should not be at the expense of the longer-term effects that may well be more important.

Harlen and Deakin Crick (2003) looked for evidence that testing raises standards and then whether testing, particularly in high stakes contexts, has a negative impact on motivation for learning that affects preparation for lifelong learning. They found that there was evidence to substantiate concerns about the impact of summative assessment on motivation for learning. Additionally they report that increase in test scores over time is likely to be due to increased familiarity of teachers and children with the tests rather than increased learning. Furthermore teachers focus on the test content, training children how to pass tests, and adopting teaching styles that do not match the preferred learning style of many children (2003, p170). This has the effect of squeezing out formative assessment.

'Teaching to the test' is a natural reaction to the desire to improve child performance and gain better overall results within a school. No amount of 'preaching' about not teaching to the test is likely to affect the practice. However, perhaps teachers need to better understand how they can effectively focus on the required learning, while at the same time maintaining teaching and learning styles that do motivate and reinforce important aspects of subject knowledge within the National Curriculum. This is where Sturman's article provides some guidance.

Personal response

Refer to your notes about how your school prepares children for National Tests and look at the extract above:

- which of the noted test preparation strategies can you identify in your teaching or in the practice of a school known to you? How does each type manifest itself?
- what effect do you think each identified type has on children?

Note down your conclusions.

Practical implications and activities

- Talk to children in Year 5 and Year 6 about their experience of science in school. Talk to them about how they feel about science and explore their attitude towards science. Note down something about their attitudes towards science as they come to the end of their time in school and find out what has influenced them.
- Ask teachers what beliefs underpin their practice in Years 5 and 6.
- Is there a pattern? What conclusions can you draw from your investigation?

How will your findings inform your beliefs about how to prepare children for national testing at Key Stages 1 and 2?

What are the implications for your practice?

Further reading

Ward, H, Roden, J, Hewlett, C and Foreman, J (2005) *Teaching science in the primary classroom.* London: PCP. Chapters 7, 8 and 9 provide many practical examples of how teachers can use stories, games and role-play and drama to promote effective learning in and motivation for learning science.

References

Armstrong, H E (1902) 'Training in scientific method as a central motive in elementary schools', Van Praagh, G (ed.) (1973) *H E Armstrong and science education.* London: John Murray.

Asoko, H (2002) 'Developing conceptual understanding in primary science', *Cambridge Journal of Education*, 32 (2). London: Taylor & Francis Ltd.

Black, P and Wiliam, D (1998) *Inside the black box: raising standards through classroom assessment.* London: Kings College London.

Black, P and Wiliam, D (2003) 'In praise of educational research: formative assessment', *British Educational Research Journal*, 29 (5).

Bybee, R W (1997) 'Achieving scientific literacy from purposes to practice'. New York: Heinemann cited in Murphy *et al.* (2001).

Craft, A (2003) 'The limits to creativity in education: dilemma for the educator', *British Journal of Educational Studies*, 51(2).

DES (1988) *Education Reform Act.* London: HMSO.

DES (1989) *National Curriculum: Non-Statutory guidance.* London: HMSO.

DfEE (1999) *Science: the National Curriculum for England.* London: DfEE.

DfES (2002) *Qualifying to teach: professional standards for Qualified Teacher Status and requirements for Initial Teacher Training.* London: TTA.

DfES (2003) *Every child matters.* London: DfEE.

DfES (2003) *Excellence and enjoyment: a strategy for primary schools.* Nottingham: DfES.

DfES/TTA (2002) *Qualifying to teach: professional standards for Qualified Teacher Status.* London: DfES/TTA.

Duggan, S and Gott, R (2002) 'What sort of science education do we really need?', *International Journal of Science Education*, 24 (7). London: Taylor & Francis Ltd.

Galton, M *et al.* (1980) *Inside the primary classroom.* London: Routledge and Kegan Paul.

Galton, M (2002) 'Continuity and progression in science teaching at Key Stages 2 and 3', *Cambridge Journal of Education*, 32 (2).

Hallam, S, Ireson, J, and Davies, J (2004) 'Primary pupils' experiences of different types of grouping in school', *British Educational Research Journal*, 30 (4).

Hallam, S, Ireson, J, Lister, V, and Chaudhury, I A (2003) 'Ability grouping practices in the primary school: a survey', *British Educational Research Journal*, 29 (1).

Hargreaves, D H (1967) *Social relations in a secondary school.* London: Tinling.

Harlan, W and Qualter, A (2004) 'The goals of learning science', chapter 6 in *The teaching of science in primary schools.* London: David Fulton.

Harlen, W and Winter, J (2004) 'The development of assessment for learning: learning from the case of science and mathematics', *Language Testing*, 21 (3). London: Hodder Arnold Journals.

Lacey, C (1970) *Hightown Grammar.* Manchester: Manchester University Press.

Mercer, N, Dawes, L, Wegerif, R and Sams, C (2004) 'Reasoning as a scientist: ways of helping children to use language to learn science', *British Educational Research Journal*, 30 (3). London: Taylor & Francis Ltd.

Murphy, C and Beggs, J, Hickey, I, O'Meara, J and Sweeney, J (2001) 'National Curriculum: compulsory school science – is it improving scientific literacy?', *Educational Research*, 43 (2).

NACCE (1999) *All our futures: creativity, culture and education.* London: DfEE.

National Curriculum Council (NCC) *Science: non statutory guidance.* York: NCC.

Newton, P D and Newton, L D (2000) 'Do teachers support causal understanding through their discourse when teaching primary science?', *British Educational Research Journal,* 26 (5). London: Taylor & Francis Ltd.

Office for Standards in Education/Her Majesty's Inspectorate (OFSTED/HMI) (2005) *The national literacy and numeracy strategies and the primary curriculum.* London HMI. **www.ofsted.gov.uk**

Ovens, P (2004) 'A "SANE" way to encourage creativity', *Primary Science Review,* 81 (Jan/Feb.) Hatfield: the Association for Science Education.

Parliamentary Office of Science and Technology (2003) *Postnote primary science.* London: Parliamentary Office of Science and Technology.

Qualifications and Curriculum Authority (QCA) (1989) *Schemes of Work.* London: QCA.

QCA (1998) *Standards and Key Stage 2 English, mathematics and science. Report on the 1997 National Curriculum assessments for 11-year olds.* London: DfEE.

QCA (1999) *Standards and Key Stage 2 English, mathematics and science. Report on the 1998 National Curriculum assessments for 11-year olds.* London: DfEE.

QCA (2000) *Curriculum guidance for the Foundation Stage (CGFS).* London: QCA.

QCA (2001) *Standards at Key Stage 2, English, mathematics and science: a report for headteachers, class teachers and assessment coordinators on the 2000 National Curriculum assessments for 11-year-olds.* London: QCA.

QCA (2001) 'Drying sponge, Question 5'. *Key Stage 2 Science Test Paper B levels 3–5.* London: QCA (Enterprises) Ltd.

QCA (2002) 'Bathtime, Question 5'. *Key Stage 2 Science Test Paper A, levels 3–5.* London: QCA (Enterprises) Ltd.

QCA (2003a) *Assessing progress in science: teacher's guide.* London: QCA (Enterprises) Ltd.

QCA (2003b) 'Evaporation, Question 5'. *Key Stage 2 Science Test Paper B, levels 3–5.* London: QCA (Enterprises) Ltd.

QCA (2004) *National Curriculum Tests 2004: Implications for teaching and learning from the 2004 tests.* London: QCA.

QCA (2004) 'The water cycle, Question 9'. *Key Stage 2 Science Test Paper B, levels 3–5,* London: QCA (Enterprises) Ltd.

QCA (2005a) *National Curriculum Tests 2004: implications for teaching and learning from the 2004 tests.* London: QCA (Enterprises) Ltd.

QCA (2005b) 'Washing day', Question 2'. *Key Stage 2 Science Test Paper A, levels 3–5.* London: QCA (Enterprises) Ltd.

Qualter, A (1996) 'Grouping in science', *Differentiated primary science.* Buckingham: Open University Press.

Ratcliffe, M (1998) 'The purposes of science education', chapter 1.1 in Sherrington, R (ed.) *ASE Guide to Primary Science Education.* Hatfield: ASE/Stanley Thornes.

Robinson, W P (2004) 'Single-sex teaching and achievement in science', *International Journal of Science Education,* 14 May 26 (6). London: Taylor & Francis Ltd.

Roden, J (1991) 'The effects on students of students simulating the role of science co-ordinator in the primary classroom.' Unpublished MA (Ed) Thesis University of Liverpool.

Roden, J (2003) 'Bridging the gap: the role of the science co-ordinator in improving the induction and professional growth of Newly Qualified Teachers', *Journal of In-service Education,* 29 (2).

Roden, J and Ward, H (2005) 'What is science?', chapter 1 in Ward, H *et al. Teaching science in the primary classroom: a practical guide.* London: Sage Publications Ltd.

Russell, T (1998) 'What the Standard tests tell us about learning science' in Sherrington, R (ed.), *ASE Guide to Primary Science Education.* Hatfield: ASE/Stanley Thornes.

Rutledge, N (2004) 'Genesis of the ice trolls', *Primary Science Review,* 81 (Jan/Feb). Hatfield: The Association for Science Education.

Science Processes and Concepts Exploration (SPACE) (Various) Research Reports Liverpool: Liverpool University Press.

Sears, J and Sorensen, P (2000) *Issues in Science Education,* London: RoutledgeFalmer.

Sherrington, R (ed.) (1988) *ASE guide to Primary Science Education,* Hatfield: ASE/ StanleyThornes.

Stringer, J (2003) 'Is this a fair test?', *Times Educational Supplement,* 21 February. **www.tes.co.uk/search/story/?story.id=375827** accessed 7 June 2005.

Sturman, L (2003) 'Teaching to the test: science or intuition', *Educational Research,* 45 (3 Winter). London: Taylor & Francis Ltd.

Topping, K J, Peter, C, Stephen, P and Whele, M (2004) 'Cross-age peer tutoring of science in the primary school: influence on scientific language and thinking', *Educational Psychology,* 24 (1). London: Carfax (Taylor & Francis Ltd).

Torrance, H and Pryor, J (2001) 'Developing formative assessment in the classroom: using action research to explore and modify theory', *British Educational Research Journal,* 27 (5). London: Carfax (Taylor & Francis Ltd).

Van Praagh, G (ed.) (1973) *H. E. Armstrong and scientific education,* London: John Murray.

Ward, H (2005) 'Scientific enquiry', chapter 5, Ward, H, Roden, J, Hewlett, C and Foreman, J (2005) *Teaching science in the primary classroom: a practical guide.* London: Sage Publications Ltd.

Watson, R, Goldsworthy, A and Wood-Robinson, V (2000) 'Sc1 beyond the fair test', chapter 8, Sears, J and Sorensen, P. *Issues in Science Education.* London: RoutledgeFalmer.

Wellington, J (1998) 'Reasons for doing practical work now – and their limitations', *Practical work in school science: which way now?* London: Routledge.

Wenham, M (2005) 'The relevance of scientific investigation', *Understanding primary science: ideas, concepts and explanations* (2nd Edition). London: Sage Publications Ltd.

Index

Armstrong, HE
  scientific method, on, 38-9. *see also* Practical
  work, role of
Assessment
  formative. *see* Formative assessment
  purposes of 86
  summative. *see* Summative assessment
Causal understanding 66-9
Children's ideas 56-69
  alternative frameworks 56-7
  causal understanding 67-9
    classroom priorities, and 67-8
    construction of 68
    discussion and conclusions 67-9
    high level of interaction between
      teacher and children 68
    making mental connections 66-7
    understanding, definition 66
    understanding, importance of 66
  challenging 64
  'content of science', acquisition of 64
  cross-curricular approach, need for 64
  developing conceptual understanding in
    primary science 56-9
  discussion 58
  learning science, long term process
    as 57
  need for new ideas 57
  questions to guide planning piece of
    teaching 57
  teaching science concepts 57
  translating knowledge into strategies for
    teaching 56-8
  use of children's initial ideas 58
  development of procedural understanding,
    need for 68
  flexibility, need for 60
  making up 'wrong' idea 59-60
    examples of young children's ideas 60
  misconceptions 56-7
    everyday experiences, and 56-7
  nature of 56
  reasoning as a scientist 62-4
    discussion and conclusions 64
    doubtful quality of collaborative talk 62-3
    intervention programme 63
    peer-group interaction 62-3
    scientific education as discursive
      process 61-3
    talk-focused classrooms 64
    use of language 62-3
  research into 58-9
  valuing understanding 68
  working with 59
Choice, need for 46
Classifying and identifying 52
Concepts
  teaching science 57
Conceptual understanding, 45. *see also* Children's
  ideas
Content of science
  providing opportunities for pupils to
    acquire 64-5
Convergent assessment 94

Decisions table 53-4
Developing systems 52
Diagnostic assessment 86
Divergent assessment 94

Elicitation 87
Experience
  art of gaining 38-9
Exploration
  orientation, and 87
Exploring 52

Fair testing 52
Flexibility
  using children's ideas, and 60
Formative assessment 84-96
  applying principles of 88
  assessing progress in science teachers guide 85-8
    assessing progress in science flowchart
      87
    benefits of formative assessment 86
    children's reflection 88
    diagnostic assessment 86
    elicitation 87
    exploration and orientation 87
    'in a nutshell' message 85
    intervention 87
    learning agenda 87
    message to teachers implicit in 85
    purposes of assessment 86
    teacher reflection 88
    'teaching and learning' 86
  decline of in late 1980s 85
  developing 93-4
    convergent assessment 94
    divergent assessment 94
    'ideal-typical' approaches 93
  development of assessment for learning
    90-2
    development of conceptual
      understanding 91
    lists of behaviours indicating
      progression 91
    questioning and listening 92
    stages of levels 91
    using indicators of progress 90-1
  'focusing frame' 92
  functions served by 84
  fundamental nature of assessment 88
  Piagetian theory, emphasis on 84
  research informing 95
  'start where the children are' 88
  targets 95
  using skills of enquiry 92

Group work
  importance of 7
Grouping children 78-83
  ability, by 71
  cross-age peer tutoring of science 79-81
    improved attitudes to science, and 81
    previous studies of paired science 81
    theoretical advantages of 79
  effect of belonging to social group 70

grouping at micro level, effect 70-1
grouping in science 71-2
  ability, by 72
    judging ability in science, concerns with
      73
    reasons for 72
    seating 72
  most effective arrangement for optimum
    learning 73
  observation of children's interaction in
    class 78
    investigative questions 78
  paired children, qualitative informal
    observations of 82
  parental involvement, and 82
    practicalities involved in 82
  peer tutoring 82
    arguments against 82
  qualitative evidence 78
  quantitative data, use of 78
  single-sex teaching and achievement in
    science 75-8
    attitudes of children to SS teaching 78-9
    chlidren's comments 78
    concern about boys' lower achievement
      75
    differences between girls and boys 75
    idea of arranging for SS classes 75
    qualitative data 76
    teachers comments 76
  why pupils are grouped differently for
    science 73

Ideas
  children's. see Children's ideas
  developing 11-12
  scientific. see Scientific ideas
Imaginative power
  absence of
    role of practical work, and 39
Indicators of progress
  using 90-1
Intervention 87
Intervention programme 63
Investigating models 51

Key Stage 2 Science Test Paper A 104-11

Language
  use in learning science 62-4
Listening 92

Making things 51-2
Misconceptions 56-7
  children's everyday experiences, and 56-7

National curriculum
  aspects of scientific enquiry within 43
  guidance on implementation of 18
  recommendations for curricular reform 46
Nuclear power 6

Orientation
  exploration, and 87

Pairing children
  benefits of 82
Parental involvement
  grouping children, and 82
Pattern-seeking 52

Peer group interaction 62-3
Peer tutoring 81
Philosophy of science
  exploring 13
Piagetian theory 84
Planning
  skill of 12
Practical work, role of 33-42
  Armstrong, HE, on 38-40
    context of writing 40
    exploration of word science 40
    role of teacher 40
  justification for inclusion of scientific
    investigation 42
  nature of the practical 36
  reasons for doing 34-6
    affective arguments 35
    cognitive arguments 35
    skills arguments 35
    small group work, benefits of 36
    three main areas 35
  relevance of scientific investigation 41-2
  reluctance to undertake practical work 33
  role in learning science 38-9
    absence of imaginative power 39
    central motive 38
    obtaining answers by experimenting 39
    role of teacher 39
    science, meaning 38-9
  scientific enquiry, and 33
Primary curriculum
  science as important part of 13
Procedural understanding 45
Process skills
  role of 43

Questioning 92

Reflection
  children's 88
  teacher 88

Science
  application to contemporary issues 6
  contribution to school curriculum 15-17
  creative activity, as 20-32
    accessible and relevant learning context
      25
    alternative view of 'creative teaching' 30-1
    appropriate learning context 26
    authenticity of questions 29
    changes to curriculum, and 20
    child making 'right' connection 31
    'creativity', association with arts 20
    distinction between creative teaching
      and teaching for creativity 31
    drafting phase, and 21
    encouraging children to be creative in
      science 29-30
    financial need for development of new
      ideas 22
    fun learning context 25
    history of science, and 21
    imaginative planning in response to
      assessments of children's ideas 26
    justifications for 'fun' approach 26
    leap of the imagination 22
    motivation, and 27
    need for creative scientists 22
    need for more scientists 23

need for stimulating environment 31
perception as 'objective' 20
processes of creativity 21
reasons to teach creatively 27
risk 31
role for primary teacher 23
'SANE' way to encourage creativity 29-30
science as convergent activity 20
teaching should not seek to provide
    entertainment 27
treating questions as emergent
    objectives 29-30
turning questions into plans for
    scientific enquiry 29-30
very young children 31-2
where creativity can enhance learning
    25
cross-curricular approach to teaching 65
elements of, diagram 17
exploration of nature of 13
four threads of 10-11
importance of 3
important part of primary curriculum, as
    13
meaning of word 38-9
national curriculum non-statutory
    guidance (NCC 1989), on 18
philosophy of. see Philosophy of science
public understanding of
    five categories of arguments for 16-17
qualities needed to solve scientific problem
    11
reasons for studying 4-5
school, in. see School science
understanding contribution of to society 18
Science education
    benefits of experience of 15-16
    purposes of 14-15
Scientific enquiry 43-55
    aspects with National Curriculum 47
    content of primary science 47
    development of procedural understanding
        49-50
    importance of 48-50
        choice 49
        common approach across school 49
        focus of science teaching 48
        stages of scientific enquiry 48-9
        'what to do' and 'how to do it' 49
    internet, and 47
    issues in science education 51-4
        children's response to investigations 52-3
        decisions table for zoo visit 53-4
        investigative approaches 52
        kinds of investigations 52
        lack of comprehension of educational
            aims of investigation 53
        model of investigative processes 52
        restriction of children's choices 53
        six kinds of investigations 52
    key issues to be explored 46
    lack of teacher awareness about learning
    intentions 54-5
    need for child choice 50
    need for staff development 54
    questioning validity of scientific 'truths' 46
    range of activities that make up 54
    role of process skills 43
    sort of science education needed 44-6
        conceptual understanding 45-6

implications for science education 45
problems with content of science
    curriculum 44
procedural understanding 45
recommendations for curricular reform
    46
Scientific ideas
    nature of 12
Scientific investigation
    kinds of 52
    relevance of 41-2
Scientific literacy
    contribution of primary science to 5
    need for all future citizens to have 5
    overall aim 4-5
    understading of term 6
    use of term 4
Scientific understanding
    nature of 12-13
Single sex (SS) teaching. see Grouping children
Summative assessment 97-116
    analysis of child performance 100-1
    analysis of questions 112
    change in National Curriculum test items
        98
    change in practice, and 98
    experimental and investigative science,
        assessment of 97
        outcomes of non-inclusion of tests items
            97
    implications from 2004 tests 98-100
        curriculum and standards 100
        examples of progress 99
        Key Stage 2 Science 98-9
        Sc1 Scientific enquiry 99
        Sc2 life processes and living things 99
        Sc3 materials and their properties 100
        Sc4 physical processes 100
    Key Stage 2 Science Test Paper A 104-9
    practical context 101
    teaching to the test 113-5
        analysis of frequencies 114-5
        'teaching to the test' 116
        'test preparation' 113
    understanding of ideas 112

Teacher
    role of 41
'Teaching to the test' 113-5
Test preparation 114

Understanding
    conceptual. see Children's ideas
    definition 67
    importance of 67
    need for focus on procedural 68

Wind generation 6
'Wrong' ideas 60